Robert Douglas

Li Hungchang

Robert Douglas

Li Hungchang

ISBN/EAN: 9783337113445

Printed in Europe, USA, Canada, Australia, Japan

Cover: Foto ©Andreas Hilbeck / pixelio.de

More available books at **www.hansebooks.com**

LI

HUNGCHANG

By

PROF. ROBERT K. DOUGLAS

LONDON

BLISS, SANDS AND FOSTER

CRAVEN STREET, STRAND

1895

PREFACE

THE biographer of a Chinese statesman is at a distinct disadvantage compared with the writer of the life of a European notability. For him no kind friends produce packets of letters, in which the subject of the biography has expressed his thoughts and opinions for the benefit of his friends and relations. No diaries are forthcoming, in which is recorded the passage of events, with criticisms upon them; nor does any literary acquaintance lighten the labours of the biographer by publishing personal reminiscences. So far as the outside world is concerned, a Chinese statesman appears only in the light of a public character. He is never to be seen but *en grande tenue*, and is to be met with only at formal interviews and public functions. The line of demarcation between the mandarin and the man is clearly defined, and he is only to be followed into the domestic retreats of his household by the help of the tongue of gossip.

The complete separation which is insisted upon between the sexes would, under any circumstances, make social intercourse, in the European sense, impossible; and the ill-will which unhappily exists on the part of the mandarins towards foreigners, forms an impassable barrier in the way of even such friendly interchange of courtesies as the maimed conditions of society allow.

The materials for the present life of Li Hung-chang have been gathered from every available source—from the *Peking Gazette*, in which Li is in the habit of constantly expressing to his lord and master his views on political and administrative questions, and in the pages of which he receives outspoken praise or blame, as the circumstances may determine, from the imperial pencil; from the local newspapers, which chronicle his comings, goings, and doings with all the accuracy in their power; from Blue Books, in which Li's part in all the diplomatic controversies of the time are recorded; and from friends who have been brought into close and frequent contact with the great Viceroy.

Experience has shown that one word is necessary

as to the pronunciation of the name Li Hungchang. For those who are unacquainted with the usually accepted system of transcribing Oriental names, it may be a convenience to know that the name is best phonetically expressed on paper as Lee Hoongchâng, the *â* being pronounced as *a* in *father.*

ROBERT K. DOUGLAS.

June 7th, 1895.

CONTENTS

CHAPTER I.

CHAPTER II.

CHAPTER III.

CHAPTER IV.

CHAPTER V.

CHAPTER VI.

CHAPTER VII.

CHAPTER VIII.

CHAPTER IX.

LIST OF ILLUSTRATIONS

CHRONOLOGICAL TABLE

1822 Birth of Li Hungchang.
1849 Admission to the Hanlin College.
1851 Outbreak of the T'aip'ing Rebellion.
1853 Capture of Nanking by the T'aip'ings.
1859 Li promoted to the rank of Taot'ai.
1862 Appointed Governor of Kiangsu.
1863 Recapture of Soochow and massacre of the Wangs.
1864 Recapture of Nanking.
1865 Outbreak of the Nienfei Rebellion.
1865 Li appointed to act against the Nienfei.
1867 Appointed Viceroy of Hukwang.
1868 Degraded for apathy before the Rebels.
1869 Made a *Tsaihsiang*, or Cabinet Minister.
1870 Tientsin massacre.
1870 Li appointed Viceroy of Chihli.
1872 Li's alarm at Japanese reforms.
1873 Signs treaty with Japan.
1874 Formosan difficulty with Japan.
1875 Death of Emperor and Empress.
1875 Li appointed Grand Secretary.
1875 Murder of Margary.
1876 Li signs Chefoo Convention.
1876 Kwo's visit to England.
1877 The great famine.
1878 The Kuldja difficulty.
1880 Gordon's visit to Li.
1882 Death of Li's mother.
1882 Outbreak in Korea.
1884 Outbreak of hostilities in Tongking.

1884	The Fournier treaty.
1885	Renewed disturbances in Korea.
1885	Treaty between China and Japan.
1886	Treaty between China and France.
1886	Occupation of Port Hamilton.
1887	Rendition of Port Hamilton.
1888	Marriage of Li's daughter.
1888	Li has a stroke of paralysis.
1892	His seventieth birthday.
1892	Death of his wife.
1894	Outbreak of war with Japan.
1894	(July 25) Sinking of the *Kowshing*.
1894	(July 30) Battle of Asan.
1894	(Sept. 15) Battle of Pingyang.
1894	(Nov. 21) Fall of Port Arthur.
1894	(Nov. 27) Mr. Detring's Mission arrives in Japan.
1895	(Jan. 26) Chang and Shao sent as Ambassadors.
1895	(Feb. 7) Fall of Wei-hai-wei.
1895	(Feb. 12) Admiral Ting commits suicide.
1895	(Mar. 16) Li goes as Plenipotentiary to Japan.
1895	(April 17) Signs the Treaty.
1895	(May 8) Ratifications exchanged at Chefoo.

LI HUNGCHANG.

CHAPTER I

His birth and family history—Madame Li—Li's early career—Rise
of the T'aip'ing rebellion—The Triad Society—Hung Siuts'uan—
T'aip'ing victories—Li's first active services—His appearance—
Appointed to Fuhkien—Fall of Hangchow and Soochow—Attack
on Shanghai.

SEVENTY-THREE years ago there was born at
Hofei, in the province of Anhui, a man who was
destined to exercise a wider influence on the home and
foreign policies of China than any other man of the
present century. After the stay-at-home manner of
Chinese classes, the family of Li had resided at Hofei
for countless generations. Their lot in life had not been
remarkable, and the head of the family, the father of the
present Viceroy of Pechihli, was not distinguished either
by wealth or by commanding intellect. He had, it is
true, gained a bachelor's degree at the examination halls,
but possessing neither interest nor money, he was content
to take his place among the unemployed members of the
Literati class. Of Madame Li we know nothing, but it
may be assumed from the fact of two of her five sons,
the subject of this biography being the second, having

acquired Viceregal rank, that she was a woman of unusual
ability. Very little is recorded of Li Hungchang's youth
beyond the fact that he was studious, and that at an early
age he acquired the habit of writing the complex characters
of his country with a beauty and exactness which gained
him marked distinction among his fellows. The same
exquisite penmanship is his at the present day, and
though such matters in Western lands are of small
account, among Eastern peoples, and especially among
the Chinese, a scholarly hand is regarded as a ready
title to honour.

When still young Li Hungchang took his bachelor
degree, and subsequently competed successfully for higher
literary honours both at the provincial capital and at
Peking. At the final schools he acquitted himself so well
that he was admitted into the Hanlin College—an institution which holds much the same sort of place with
regard to literature as the Royal Society does among
ourselves in scientific matters. But it has this advantage
over the English body, that the graduates receive certain
salaries, in return for which it becomes their duty to
further by every means in their power the advance of
learning. As a rule a graduate of the Hanlin College
receives, according to the rota of the academy, an appointment in the public service. Such would in ordinary
circumstances have probably been the course pursued in
Li Hungchang's case. But the times were out of joint,
and his energies were destined to be used in a wider
and more active field than commonly falls to the lot of
Chinese civilians.

For many years the southern provinces of the Empire

had been in a disturbed condition. The Hunghwui, or Triad Society, which is the most powerful of the secret associations which the Chinese government has to fear, had been actively recruiting its ranks, and had been preparing to measure its strength with the local forces of the government. The professed object of the Society was to overthrow the ruling Manchu dynasty, and to restore the throne to a representative of the Chinese people. Seditious opinions were scattered far and wide among the natives by agents of the Hunghwui, and constant outbreaks occurred, in which the government troops were not always successful. At such unruly times the appearance of a leader is all that is needed to give head to the revolutionary ideas prevailing. Such a man arose in the person of a student in the province of Kwangtung, who adopted the surname Hung to mark his association with the Society, and the personal name of Siuts'uan as being of felicitous import. This man, who was destined to achieve a temporary greatness, was born in 1813 in a small village not many miles from Canton. His father was an agriculturist, and the early days of the future Tien Wang, or Heavenly Prince, were spent in herding cattle on the farm. On reaching manhood he rebelled against this prosaic calling, and exchanged it for the not much more exciting office of village schoolmaster.

But his ambition was still unsatisfied, and he presented himself on several occasions before the examiners at Canton, hoping to obtain a footing in official life. His literary acquirements, however, were not sufficient to procure for him his degree, and to his repeated failures must doubtless be attributed the direction which his

energies ultimately took.   On one of his visits to Canton
he met a Protestant missionary, from whose agents he
received a number of Christian tracts.   Some of these
he read, and though he failed to understand them aright,
they exercised a powerful influence on his diseased imagination.   Overwork and disappointment brought on a
serious attack of illness, in the course of which he saw
visions in which God the Father and God the Son
appeared, and exhorted him to take up arms against the
Manchu rulers of his country.   Among an ignorant people
a seer of visions is commonly regarded as one beloved
of the gods, more especially when his dreams happen to
accord with the current feelings of his neighbours.

With the zeal of an enthusiast Hung Siuts'uan set about
converting his friends and acquaintances to the pseudo-
Christianity which the tracts and visions had taught him.
With indefatigable energy he and his disciples travelled
through the provinces of Kwangtung and Kwangsi preach-
ing the new faith, which was cunningly shaped so as to
include revolutionary doctrines.   By these means he
gathered some thousand followers to his standards, and
at a given signal he led them against a neighbouring
market town, which readily fell into his hands.   This
victory was followed up by the capture of other places,
and on the 27th August, 1851, he captured the city of
Yungan (Eternal Peace).   Fortune at first attached herself
to his standards.   He marched a conquering army of
ten thousand men through the province of Hunan, and
in the beginning of 1853 captured Nanking, on the
Yangtsze-Kiang.   This city, which had been the capital
of the Empire under the Ming dynasty, was immediately

proclaimed the imperial city of the new T'aip'ing (Great Peace) dynasty, which the Tien-Wang believed himself ordained to establish. Unhappily for him he seemed to forget in his triumph that his success was only half won, and instead of marching with the prestige of victory northwards on Peking, he employed his troops in expeditions on the banks of the river, and devoted his energies to establishing a complicated system of civil government. Four of his most faithful followers, Fêng, Yang, Siao, and Wei were severally appointed kings of the south, east, west, and north, while at subsequent periods he nominated other kings, as the spirit moved him. With the absence of all immediate incentives to exertion a complete change came also over his personal habits. He retired within the precincts of his palace, where he was waited upon by women only, and to which admittance was only granted to his most trusted followers. Few particulars of the life which he led at this period were allowed to circulate, but incidentally facts became public which showed that he had fallen completely into the enervating mode of life common to Eastern potentates.

On one occasion, Yang, the eastern king, who was subject to trances, had, or thought he had, a message from the Almighty ordering him to rebuke and chastise the T'ien-Wang for his treatment of the women within the palace. Yang, who appeared to be by no means loth to exercise the delegated authority thus granted him, took his chief to task, and even induced him to prostrate himself to receive the chastisement decreed by the Most High. This humiliation was considered to be sufficient, and Yang, instead of inflicting the merited stripes, proceeded to remonstrate with him on the gross impropriety of kicking and otherwise ill-using his concubines and female attendants. For a time the T'ien-Wang submitted to these rebukes, and even proclaimed Yang to be the personification of the Holy Ghost. But at last the yoke became unendurable, and on a charge of treachery, which ill-became his divine character, Yang was tried, condemned, and beheaded.

Meanwhile bands of T'aip'ings advanced down the river and captured Chinkiang and Yangchow without firing a shot, the garrisons of those places flying before their enemies with an alacrity quite equal to that which the Chinese troops have lately shown in the presence of their Japanese foes. Having looted everything worth taking in these cities, they carried off the inhabitants to Nanking. By these and similar expedients they raised the number of their fighting men to about a hundred thousand, and employed even the captured women in the construction of fortifications for the further protection of the city. But the necessity of an advance on Peking was not entirely forgotten, and in May, 1853, a column was despatched northwards. With varying success it marched through the provinces of Anhui, Honan, Shantung, Southern Chihli, and finally captured the city of Tsinghai, some twenty miles from Tientsin.

It was at this time that Li Hungchang, who was residing at his father's house at Hofei, first emerged from the literary world to take part in the national strife. The presence of the T'aip'ings in his native province roused his patriotic ardour, and recognising that it was a time when every man who had any influence or authority should exercise it to the utmost for his country's weal, he raised a regiment of militia and led them into the field against the foe. With the means at his command he could not do much more than harrass the T'aip'ings. Any brilliant victory was beyond his reach, but as the rebels advanced northwards he was able to do some service by hanging on their rear and cutting off stragglers. But with the disappearance of the first column across the frontier into Honan his work was by no means ended, for shortly afterwards a second column marched through the province into Shantung and captured the important city of Lintsing. If the first column had succeeded in holding its own at Tsinghai, it is quite possible that with the assistance of the second army it might have affected the capture of Peking. But both advances were too much in the nature of raids. The armies marched through the country as isolated bodies, cut off entirely from their bases, and closely followed up by the Imperial forces. Movement, therefore, was essential to their success, and when the advance guard received a check before Tientsin, the fate of the column was sealed. After enduring a siege of some months at Tsinghai, the T'aip'ings, starving and desperate, cut their way through the Imperial lines and marched south to Nanking. The news of this retreat induced the commander of the second column to follow suit, and though Li Hungchang with his militia was on the alert he was quite unable to bar the retreat. The useful work he had been able to do, however, was sufficient to attract the attention of Tsêng Kwofan, the Viceroy of Hukwang and generalissimo of the army, who enlisted Li and his men among the troops under his immediate command. The result fully justified the general's selection, and Li ably carried out the warlike expeditions and military work entrusted to him.

Though a civilian by training Li has many of the qualities of a soldier. In physique he stands head and shoulders above the average height of his countrymen, measuring more than six feet. His eyes, which are not even yet dimmed by age, are bright, piercing, and sparkling. His manner is calm and collected, and his features indicate ability and tenacity of purpose. Tsêng Kwofan was unquestionably the ablest man of his time, and Li must with equal certainty rank next to him. In rapid succession he rose from rank to rank, until in 1859 he was sent to Fuhkien in the office of Taotai or intendent of circuit. This is always an office of importance, but more especially was it so at that time, when the T'aip'ings were actively recruiting their ranks from among the unruly population in the province. Here Li discharged his duties with the same fidelity and vigour as he had displayed in Anhui. His absence from the Central Provinces was, probably, of less moment at that time than at any other period, for the rebellion was apparently on its last legs. Nanking was closely besieged, and the garrison were compelled to resort "to every possible means of sustaining life short of eating human flesh," while the other cities in the possession of the rebels were hardly pressed by the Imperial forces. The war with England and France in 1860, however, changed all this, and gave a new impetus to the T'aip'ings by paralyzing the efforts of the Imperialists. One man among the rebel leaders stands

out prominently for the vigour and success with which he
opposed Li Hungchang. Throughout his whole career
Chung Wang, or the Faithful King, showed undaunted
courage in battle, and marked fertility of resource. To
his efforts, following on the foreign war, is chiefly to be
attributed the revival of the rebellion at this period. It
had become essential to the movement that some new
districts should be absorbed, and especially that cities of
wealth and importance should be added to the kingdom
of the Heavenly Prince. Of all cities in Central China
two are pre-eminently renowned for wealth and luxury—a
reputation which finds expression in the proverbial saying,
"See Soo and Hang and die." Against these two cities,
Soochow and Hangchow, therefore, the Faithful King
directed his attack. With comparative ease he captured
Hangchow, and was proceeding to lay siege to Soochow
when he received a command from the Heavenly King to
go at once to the relief of Nanking. For a sixth time he
succeeded in raising the siege of that city, and then
returned to prosecute his campaign in the fertile plains of
Kiangsu. With all speed he marched on Soochow, and
without much difficulty added that city to his list of
conquests. Though the possession of these two important
towns added much to the strength and prestige of his
position, the king never lost sight of the fact that the
acquisition of a seaport was after all essential to the
ultimate success of the rebellion. Shanghai was at this
time well known as the greatest port and emporium of
trade in the empire. It was the point of distribution for
the central and Northern provinces, and especially for
those cities and marts lying on the shores of the Yangtsze

Kiang. The Faithful King clearly perceiving that the
possession of this town would put him into direct communication with the outer world, and would further place
him in easy touch with Nanking and the other cities which
had been captured from the Imperialists, determined to
advance against it. Subsequently he declared that he had
been urged to undertake the expedition by some of the
foreign residents, and he expressly accused the French of
having invited him. But however that may be, he
advanced to the attack with the greatest confidence, and
gained a complete victory over the Imperial forces, who
were protecting the approaches to the town. To his
surprise, however, on arriving before the city, he found the
walls manned by English and French sailors, by whom
the assaults of his troops were repulsed with considerable
loss, not once nor twice.

CHAPTER II.

AT this time Li Hungchang was serving again under his old chief Tsêng Kwofan. With that keenness of observation which has always distinguished him, he had learned to recognise the superiority of foreigners in the field and in the workshop, and while he did not for an instant admit that they were other than "barbarians," he was yet fully alive to the value of their courage, ingenuity, and technical skill. He early advised therefore that a certain number of foreigners should be enlisted to drill and lead a division of the Imperial army. The threatened attack on Shanghai by the Faithful King had greatly alarmed the native merchants of that city, who were driven by the emergency to band themselves together into a Patriotic Association for the protection of the town. They raised money for the defence, and engaged at Li's instigation an American, named Ward, who had drifted to Shanghai with the true instinct of an adventurer, to lead a force in defence of the Imperial cause. At a seaport like Shanghai there are always a number of discharged sailors and other idle hands, who

are fit for stratagems and spoils, and Ward had no
difficulty in enlisting a hundred Europeans to serve under
his banner. With this force he attacked the city of
Sungkiang, and though he was at first unsuccessful, he
eventually captured the town. The loot gained in this
enterprise was considerable, and so raised the spirits of
Ward's followers that they readily responded to a proposal
to attack the town of Tsingpu. This city was of considerable strength, and a Chinese force of ten thousand
men, with about two hundred small Chinese gunboats,
were ordered to co-operate with Ward's battalions.
Tsingpu, however, was not only a strong place, but the
defence was entrusted to an Englishman named Savage,
who so ably handled his men that with the assistance
of the Faithful King, who advanced to the relief of the
town, he completely defeated the attacking force.

The neighbourhood of the rebels to the various Treaty
Ports had attracted the attention of the British naval and
military authorities at the close of the war, and in 1861,
Admiral Hope steamed up the Yangtsze to Nanking, and
urged on the Heavenly King the necessity of his not
interfering with the Treaty Ports, if he desired to avoid
the intervention of the European Powers. The T'ien Wang
expressed his willingness to come to terms with the
Admiral, and agreed that no further attack should be
made on Shanghai during the next twelve months.
Meanwhile Ward's force, which had already adopted the
somewhat grandiloquent title of the "Ever-Victorious
Army," was, with the assistance of Li Hungchang, doing
excellent work against the T'aip'ings. Li's difficulties in
connection with this force were by no means incon-

siderable, and one of his chief anxieties was to supply
sufficient funds to meet the expenses of the battalion.
So hardly pressed was he that, even with the help of the
Patriotic Association at Shanghai, he professed to be
unable at all times to honour Ward's drafts. He, however,
was partly successful in the administration of the force,
and in 1862 his Imperial master appointed him Governor
of Kiangsu, in recognition of his services. At this time
Li resided principally at Shanghai, and while there was
party to an arrangement by which, with the approval of
the Ministers at Peking, a radius of thirty miles round
Shanghai was kept clear of rebels by the English and
French forces.

The war of 1860 had demonstrated to the Chinese
authorities, and to no one more clearly than to Li Hungchang, the superiority of the foreign military systems
over that of China, and the same government which
had lately defied the allied forces was only too glad
when peace was proclaimed to make use of them against
the T'aip'ings. It was therefore with complete satisfaction
that Li Hungchang saw Admiral Hope and General
Staveley take the field in pursuance of the arrangement
just mentioned. In conjunction with Ward these commanders recovered town after town from the dynasty of
"Great Peace," and so elated were the native troops by
the successes which had been thus gained, that they
determined to make an assault on T'aitsang, a strong city
which had passed into the possession of the T'aip'ings.
Hearing of the advance of this attacking force, the
Faithful King marched to the relief of the garrison,
and desiring to make sure of success, added a ruse to his

order of attack. He made two thousand of his men shave their heads and go into battle under the Imperial banners. No sooner had the fighting began than these men, at a given signal, turned against their supposed comrades, who being thrown into confusion by this outbreak in their midst, were easily defeated by the simultaneous onslaught of the Faithful King.

Meanwhile a rebel force was advancing upon the treaty port of Ningpo, which was defended by the English fleet under Captain Dew. Ward with his battalion was also operating in the neighbourhood. To this officer was detailed the duty of attacking the town of Tseki, and while gallantly leading his troops to the assault he received a wound from which he died two days later. Ward was undoubtedly a brave man, and he had done excellent service for the Chinese government. The news of his death was therefore received with universal regret, and every honour was paid to his memory by the authorities. It is worthy of mention that although he had only held command of the force for two years, he left behind him a fortune of fifteen thousand pounds. A Colonel Forester, also an American, being next in seniority, was on the death of Ward offered the command of the Ever-Victorious Army. But he declined the honour, and Ward's mantle fell on Henry Burgevine, of the same nationality. Almost before this officer was able to take up the command, an offer reached Li Hungchang, which might have tempted a less astute man to fall in with the proposition made. A Russian officer arrived at Shanghai with authority to place at the disposal of the Governor ten thousand Russian troops. Li had made himself

thoroughly acquainted with the recent action of the
European Powers in their relations with China, and the
study of this question had taught him to regard with
a profound distrust any proposition emanating from
St. Petersburg. Unquestionably ten thousand European
troops, ably led, would have settled the rebellion ; but
Li saw, or thought he saw, dangers lurking in the distance
which would make the purchase even of this advantage
too costly a bargain, and he therefore declined the offer
with thanks. It is probable that Li had some misgivings
with regard to others beside the Russians. It was commonly said that Ward carried in his knapsack a regal
sceptre, which in the event of fortune and the fitting
opportunity combining to his advantage, he was prepared
to produce. Success, however, did not attend his banners
with sufficient persistency to make him dangerous. He
was too cautious to run any great risks. But with his
successor, Burgevine, the case was different. He was
endowed with a more recklessly ambitious nature, and
was from the first viewed with distrust and suspicion by
the far-seeing Li. The two men were both too masterful
and too antagonistic in their views to make a continued
alliance possible.

An occasion of falling out soon arose. An advance
was made from Soochow by Mu Wang, one of the
T'aip'ing leaders, and was opposed successfully by troops
under Li, in conjunction with the Ever-Victorious
Army. The victory was complete, and a son of the
T'aip'ing General lost his life. It is difficult to decide
which force took a leading part in the battle. Both
leaders claimed the credit of the success, and, in course

of the dispute, the ill-will that had until then been latent,
broke out into an open quarrel. It so happened that a
General Ch'êng (Ching), who had transferred his allegiance from the rebels to the Imperialists, shared with Li
his jealousy of the Ever-Victorious Army, and did his
best on this occasion to foment the quarrel between the
disputants. The distrust which had been engendered
in the mind of Li was communicated to the Patriotic
Association at Shanghai, and the members in consequence declined to continue to pay the large sums
which they had hitherto contributed towards the maintenance of the Ever-Victorious Army. Thirty thousand
pounds a month was a sum which Li and the Association had been compelled to subscribe for the
maintenance of the force, and both the Governor and
the members of the Association felt that if they were
obliged to pay such considerable amounts, they were at
least entitled to the services of a General in whom they
could put implicit confidence. Burgevine was not such a
man, and Li determined to take active steps to depose
him. With this object in view he visited General
Staveley, then in command of the British troops at
Shanghai, and begged him to remove Burgevine, on the
several grounds of the extravagance of the force, of the
insulting behaviour of the commander towards the
Chinese authorities, and of the very loose discipline
with which he controlled his men. General Staveley
professed himself unable to take the step proposed, but
undertook to communicate with the British Minister at
Peking and the Home Government on the subject.

Meanwhile an event occurred which precipitated an

irreconcilable breach between Li and Burgevine. The pay of the men in the Ever-Victorious Army was undeniably in arrear, and Takee, a Shanghai banker and a prominent member of the Patriotic Association, through whose hands all disbursements were made to the force, had, probably owing to the growing suspicions of Burgevine's intentions, withheld a payment which he had positively undertaken to make. Burgevine was not a man to submit to the non-payment of funds due to him, and his quarrel with Li still less inclined him to endure Takee's refusal to loosen his purse strings. He therefore went with his body guard to Shanghai, and after a stormy interview with Takee, during which he used personal violence towards the banker, he carried off a very considerable sum of money, which he found on the premises. This outrage furnished Li with a further valid reason for demanding his resignation, and he now appealed to General Staveley to arrest the offender. This General Staveley had no authority to do, but he undertook to communicate to Burgevine the fact that Li had dismissed him from his command. With unexpected submission Burgevine retired from his post, and Staveley nominated Captain Holland to the command pending the appointment of a permanent chief. The news of Burgevine's dismissal was received by the Ever-Victorious Army with loud murmurs of disapprobation. The loose discipline which had prevailed under his rule, and which had afforded abundant opportunities for looting, had made him popular among the troops, and Li was seriously apprehensive of a mutiny, unless something could be done to keep both officers and men

steadfast to the colours. With a true instinct he gauged
the real cause of the discontent, and promptly recovered
their loyalty by the instant payment in full of all
arrears due.

Burgevine, however, declined to regard himself as dismissed, and only agreed to consider himself off duty
pending a reference on the whole question to the Tsungli
Yamên and the British Minister at Peking. In the
meantime Captain Holland, of General Staveley's staff,
went up to Sungkiang to take the reins until Major
Gordon, the officer whom General Staveley designed for
the appointment, should be able to assume the command.
It had been plain to all observers that for some time Li's
suspicions of the force had prompted a desire to get rid
of it altogether, and with this object in view he had, while
Burgevine was still in command, ordered him to march to
the relief of Nanking. If this march had been undertaken the force would have passed out of the province of
Kiangsu, and so beyond the limits of Li's jurisdiction.
The assumption of the command by an English officer,
however, made this expedition impossible, and Li, dis-
appointed in his main object, determined to minimise the
dangers of discontent by keeping the army constantly employed. He therefore ordered it to advance at once to the
attack of T'aitsang, a fortified town which had long been
held by the rebels. Against this venture General Staveley
protested vehemently. He told Li "that the force as yet
was not sufficiently organised to undertake such serious
affairs as the capture of walled towns." To this Li
replied that if the force could not undertake so simple
an operation it was not worth keeping up. In these

circumstances General Staveley thought it wise to allow Captain Holland to accompany the expedition, on the ground that the only hope of success lay in his presence at the attack. The result was such as General Staveley expected. The assault was completely unsuccessful, and the Ever-Victorious Army retired discomfited to Sung-kiang.

The emergency demanded instant action, and Major Gordon, who had been engaged in making a survey of the country round Shanghai, was ordered at once to take the command. From that day the fortunes of the Ever-Victorious Army appeared in the ascendant. Gordon's first expedition was against the fortified town of Fushan. "The rebel stockades were not strong, but there were heavy masses of T'aip'ings in the rear and on each flank." By the exercise of skilful manœuvring Gordon's attack was completely successful. A breach having been made in the walls, the assault was ordered, and after a paltry resistance the town fell into the hands of the Imperialists. For this achievement Gordon was made a Tsungping, or Brigadier-General, in response to a memorial addressed to the Throne by Li, who had readily recognised the superior *calibre* of his new colleague. In notifying to Major Gordon the news of his promotion, Li wrote :

"The Governor has already communicated a copy of the memorial to the Throne despatched on the 12th April from his camp at Shanghai, in which he solicited the issue of a decree conferring temporary rank as a Chinese Tsungping upon the English officer Gordon, on his taking command of the Ever-Victorious Force. He is now in the receipt of an express from the Board of War, returning his memorial with the note that a separate decree has been issued to the Prince of Kung and the Council of State ; and on the same day he received, through the Prince and Council, a copy of the decree issued to them on the 9th May in the following terms :

"'Gordon, on succeeding to the command of the Ever-Victorious Force, having displayed both valour and intelligence, and having now, with repeated energy, captured Fushan, we ordain that he at once receive rank and office as a Chinese Tsungping, and we at the same time command Li to communicate to him the expression of our approval. Let Gordon be further enjoined to use stringent efforts for maintaining discipline in the Ever-Victorious Force, which has fallen into a state of disorganization, and thus to guard against the recurrence of former evils. Respect this !'

"The Governor has accordingly to forward a copy of the foregoing Decree, to which the officer in question will yield respectful obedience."

Meanwhile Burgevine had not been idle. He had gone to Peking and had gained the good opinion of Sir Frederick Bruce, the English Minister, who strongly recommended Prince Kung to reinstate him in the command of the force. Li, however, had lost no time in expressing his views in full to the Tsungli Yamên, and Prince Kung, therefore, while courteously receiving Bruce's recommendation, declined to interfere on the ground that it was a matter within the jurisdiction of Li only. Against this Burgevine protested. He affirmed that he had been appointed by the Central Government, and that, therefore, he could only be removed by the same authority. He also stated that the circumstance of his visit to Takee had been grossly misrepresented, and he detailed his version of the interview in the following memorandum. "I left," he wrote, "at once for Shanghai, but on my arrival there next morning was coldly informed that Takee had not only denied writing the letter promising payment, but still refused to send the money. I immediately proceeded to his house with a small portion of my guard who usually accompany me. There was no forcible entrance, no confusion, the men standing quietly at 'Order Arms,' while Takee's compradore removed the money. I was aware of the responsibility of the step I was taking, but felt justified in so doing by the critical state of affairs at Sungkiang. There was no time for deliberation : it was truly a question of money or the existence of the force, and the lives of the European officers. The money had been appropriated for the use of the troops, and was immediately paid to them on its arrival at Sungkiang. The only part of the affair I regret," he added, "is having struck Takee." *

But the true cause of Li's determination to get rid of Burgevine lay, as has been said, in the suspicions he entertained with regard to that adventurer. Li, during his residence at Shanghai had gained a sufficient knowledge of foreigners to be able to differentiate them. He had no confidence whatever in Burgevine, but his communications with General Staveley and Sir Walter Medhurst, the Consul, had led him to believe that he could work harmoniously with, and implicitly trust, a British officer recommended by them for the command. It is obvious also that this predisposition was confirmed by his acquaintance with Gordon, and it is plain that throughout their whole connection, both in sunshine and in storm, for there were at times fierce quarrels between the pair, he entertained for Gordon a real esteem and friendship. The capture of Fushan and the relief of

* *Parliamentary Papers. China.* No. 3 (1864).

Changshu (Chanzu) convinced him that Gordon was a military commander of no common merit. He was, therefore, vehemently opposed to the restitution of Burgevine, and on this subject in a despatch to Vice-consul Markham, who wrote to inform him that Burgevine had received the support of the British minister at Peking, and was returning to Shanghai with an Imperial Commissioner especially deputed by the Tsungli Yamèn to settle the matter, he wrote as follows :

"The officer, Gordon, having received the command of the Ever-Victorious Army, having immediately on doing so proceeded to Fushan, working day and night, having worked harmoniously with the other generals there, having exerted himself and attacked with success the walled city, and relieved Changshu, and at once returned to Sungkiang and organized his force for further operations to sweep out the rebels, and having proved himself valiant, able, and honest, I have congratulated myself, and have memorialized His Imperial Majesty to confer on him the dignity and office of Tsungping, to enable me to consider him as part of my command.

"This Memorial I sent up on the 25th day of the 2nd moon. On the 5th of the 3rd moon I received a letter from the Tsungli Yamèn, stating that during the 2nd moon Burgevine had taken on himself to enter Peking, and proceed surreptitiously to the American Legation ; that while they were taking steps on this they received a number of letters from the American Minister, to the effect that Burgevine repented him. They also received a strong letter from the English Minister in his favour ; but that in their opinion Burgevine should be dealt with according to law for striking a mandarin, and taking forcible possession of public moneys ; but as he was guaranteed by the English and American Ministers, as he had already confessed contrition for his fault, and as he had proceeded to Shanghai, to be dealt with by the chief military authorities of the Province, they thought perhaps the rule might be departed from, and an opportunity given him to turn over a new leaf. They had, therefore, sent an officer to accompany him to Shanghai, for the Fut'ai to do what he thought best; that if Burgevine did really proceed to Shanghai, and expressed contrition for his offence, the Fut'ai might decide on the line to be taken.

"Now had a Chinaman committed the offence of which Burgevine had been guilty, he would long ere this have been seized and severely punished; but, perhaps being a foreigner, he did not fully understand Chinese customs, and he has in days gone by exerted himself in our service, and received a wound. As he has represented this at Peking, and the various foreign Ministers have spoken strongly in his favour, and as the Tsungli Yamên have written leaving the decision to me, and not distinctly ordered me to give him the command of the force should he repent him, and acknowledge his fault, I must change my course with regard to him, and not cut off entirely his chance of repairing his fault.

"But with regard to the Ward force, as when Burgevine had the command, there was no regularity about its expenses; as he allowed it to be disorderly and mutinous, disobedient to orders, and a pest to mandarins and people; as he gave no account of the manner in which he expended the 90,000 taels which Takee had got together for the Nanking expedition, and which he took thence; and as he made up claims for over 300,000 taels of debts, causing Taot'ais Woo and Yang to be degraded and involved, so that to this moment they had been unable to extricate themselves,—I cannot give him command of the force, again to increase vain expenses, and suffer future difficulties.

"Again, since Gordon has taken the command he has exerted himself to organise the force, and though he has had but one month has got the force into shape. As the people and place are charmed with him, and as he has already given me returns of the organization of the force, the formation of each regiment, and the expenses, ordinary and extraordinary, in the clearest manner,

wishing to drill our troops, and save our money, it is
evident that he fully comprehends the state of affairs,
and in the expedition he is preparing his men delightedly
obey him, and preserve proper order : I cannot therefore
remove him without cause.

"As, moreover, should the report be spread about that
Burgevine has come back to Shanghai to resume the
command, the various officers and petty officers will
be insulted, and the service will suffer, I feel it right
to make the letter I have received from the Tsungli
Yamên public, together with my intentions with regard
to it, that both Gordon may be fully satisfied as to
his position and the officers may pay no attention to
idle reports.

"I have therefore forwarded you herewith a copy of
my memorial to the Emperor, and beg you to tell Gordon
to feel every confidence, to organise the force jointly with
his Chinese colleague, to look for orders to me only, to
pay no attention to rumours and relax in consequence ;
and should any of the officers who were in the force in
Burgevine's time, and who have since been dismissed,
spread idle reports in Sung-kiang, or stir up doubts and
plots in Shanghai, causing the men to get disturbed and
mutinous, I have written to the General, to assist him to
seize and deport them, that discipline may be maintained.
The Tsungli Yamên, has, in referring Burgevine's case to
me, shown extraordinary regard for foreigners, and I
myself have no desire to show favour to one to the
disadvantage of another, at one time severe and at
another lenient, but look merely to what is best for the
armies, and least dangerous to the State. And as Gordon
carries on his duties well, I cannot displace him ; should
he not do so hereafter, I will then consider what is to be
done.   I have therefore made up my mind, and besides
replying to the Tsungli Yamên memorializing His Majesty
to settle the case, and instructing Major Gordon of my
decision, I write to inform you, and trust you will give
him similar instructions." *

* *Parliamentary Papers.   China.   No. 3 (1864).*

In the Memorial referred to in this dispatch Li laid great stress on the facts that Gordon had recovered Fushan without delaying an instant, and had worked harmoniously with him and the native Chinese generals. These facts, coupled with the powerful support which he received from Peking, confirmed Li in his determination to stand to his decision. There is no question that in this matter Li was right, and subsequent events fully justified the course he took. At this time the recovery of Soochow from the rebels was the main object which Li had in view. As a preliminary, however, it was necessary to take Kunshan (Quinsan), a strongly fortified town on the main road from T'aitsang to Soochow, and it was against this point that Gordon, in consultation with Li, directed his force in the first instance. But while yet on the road a circumstance occurred which compelled him to divert his attention at once to T'aitsang. Li had for some time been holding secret communications with the rebel leaders in that city, and had been induced by them to believe that they were willing to surrender the town. Confident in the honesty of their purpose Li despatched his brother with a force of two thousand men to arrange the terms. In fulfilment of this project General Li held several consultations with the rebel chiefs, exchanged gifts with them, and amongst other things presented on his part a number of Mandarin's hats to be worn by the rebel leaders on their joining the Imperial host. On the day appointed for the surrender (26th April) fifteen hundred Imperialist soldiers were admitted into the city. They had, however, no sooner passed within the walls than the gate by which they had entered was closed behind them and they were made prisoners, three hundred of their number being beheaded on the spot. The news of this treacherous deed led Gordon to march at once on T'aitsang, leaving the operations against Kunshan until a more convenient season. It will be remembered that T'aitsang had been the scene of a signal defeat of the Ever-Victorious Army, and the treachery of which the garrison had now been guilty added a sense of desperation to the exultation they felt at their previous victory. Gordon's force on this expedition numbered two thousand eight hundred men. He was, however, well provided with artillery, and his troops were inspired with the enthusiasm begotten of victory. Having breached the walls with his guns an assault was ordered, but the T'aip'ings fought with such gallantry that Gordon's men were driven back. A second attack proved more successful, and before night Gordon was in possession of the town.

The capture of this stronghold was followed by the occurrence of one of those events which must inevitably occur when Europeans fight side by side with Asiatics. Among the prisoners taken at T'aitsang were seven notorious rebel chiefs, who were handed over by Gordon to the custody of the Chinese general. It is not clear whether or not this officer communicated with Li on the subject of the fate of these captives, but it is clear that the inhuman punishment inflicted upon them met with his approval. Oriental ideas on the subject of punishment differ so widely from our own that it is impossible to judge them by the same rules. Following a practice not at all uncommon, the Chinese general ordered the men to be fastened to crosses, to have arrows thrust through their flesh, to have strips of skin cut off from various parts of their bodies, and in this state to be exposed till sundown and then beheaded. This barbarous sentence was carried out to the letter, and its brutality aroused a very strong feeling among the European communities in China. The Bishop of Victoria felt called upon to denounce it to Earl Russell, and the Shanghai newspapers bore eloquent testimony to the horror with which the punishment was regarded. Some of the statements made were no doubt exaggerated, but it is difficult to agree with an eye-witness on the other side, who reported that though each man had a piece of skin partly stripped from one arm and one or two arrows had been pushed through the skin in different places, the sufferers "did not appear to be in pain."

All this controversy affected Li very little. He found it difficult to understand how anyone should be disturbed at the pain inflicted on captured rebels. The punishment appeared to him to be only natural, and to be quite in accord with the best traditions of his countrymen. There is no reason to suppose that he is of a naturally cruel disposition ; although to him as to most of his countrymen the sanctity of human life has no meaning. It is said that on one occasion when he was Viceroy of Chihli a man who had been caught doing damage to a telegraph wire was brought before him. The culprit wept aloud, and repeated over and over again that he would never do it again. "Don't be vexed, my good fellow," said Li, "nor trouble yourself any further on the matter. I will take care that it shall not happen again." Then turning to the jailors he gave the simple order, "Cut off his head." But though in the case of the convicted rebels he declined

to show any concern for their fate, General Brown, who
had succeeded General Staveley in command of the
British troops at Shanghai, felt called upon to remonstrate
with him ; and gave him plainly to understand that if such
a case of inhumanity occurred again he should feel
compelled to withdraw all British officers serving with the
Imperial forces.

CHAPTER III.

HAVING thus captured T'aitsang, Gordon felt himself
at liberty to lead his force against the stronghold
of Kunshan, which strategically was the key to Soochow.
In this expedition he was associated with General Ch'êng,
who, with the usual self-confidence of Chinese commanders, had assured Li that if supplied with sufficient artillery he could at any moment make a breach
on the eastern face of the city, and capture the town.
But having made this boast he was very anxious that
Gordon should justify it for him. Gordon, however, with
the trained eye of an engineer recognised that Ch'êng had
chosen the strongest part of the line of defence for his
attack, and that the vulnerable spot was the face towards
Soochow. As a preliminary step he attacked and
captured some outworks in this direction, and then
proceeded to assault the city itself. *The Hyson*, a
steamer which was attached to the Ever-Victorious
Army, did excellent service on this occasion. A causeway connected Kunshan with Soochow, and along this

45

narrow path the vanquished rebels attempted to escape
from the doomed city. *The Hyson*, which, after proceeding up the canal towards Soochow, had turned
back on its course, faced the fugitives. Opening a fire
which enfiladed the causeway, she checked the flight of
the Taip'ings, and made terrible havoc amongst them.
It is supposed that in the engagement on that day between three and four thousand rebels were killed, while
Gordon's total loss was only two killed and five drowned.
The victory was complete, and Gordon determined to
make the captured town the headquarters of his force.
Two reasons actuated him in coming to this determination. Strategically it was obviously the most central spot
he could have chosen, and he hoped that by garrisoning it
with his troops, he might be able to wean his European
officers from some of those looser and more undisciplined
habits, which, unfortunately, characterised some of them.
The effect of the move on these men, who were brave
enough in battle, but who were contentious and unruly
when they had laid by their armour, showed him that he
was right. A mutiny broke out, and the troops refused
to parade when ordered to do so. Gordon was not a
man to brook such insubordination. He called out the
non-commissioned officers, whom he regarded as the
moving spirits in the agitation, and warned them that
unless the troops fell in before a given hour, every
fifth man among them would be shot. To encourage
the others he ordered the recognised leader of the
movement to be shot there and then, and locked up
the rest that they might have an opportunity of cogitating
on the course to be pursued. When the hour struck

they one and all begged to be restored to their posts, and the danger was over.

General Ch'êng, however, had never forgiven Gordon for departing from his scheme for carrying Kunshan, and as a mark of his displeasure he "mistook" the flag borne by a regiment of the Ever-Victorious Army, which was serving with another Imperial force, and opened fire upon it. When called to account by Gordon for this iniquity Ch'êng tried at first to treat the whole matter as a joke. But Gordon was determined that he should be made fully to understand the enormity of his crime. After writing to Li, giving him an account of Ch'êng's action and stating his determination to inflict punishment upon him, he led his troops to Ch'êng's camp. Li was greatly disturbed at this fracas. He could not but feel that Ch'êng was either a traitor or an incapable blunderer, but at the same time he recognised that he was a useful general, and he was not disposed to trust him to the tender mercies of Gordon's righteous anger. He therefore sent Dr. Macartney, now Sir Halliday Macartney, to mediate between the chiefs. With the diplomatic address, which has since gained Sir Halliday so much distinction, he brought the matter to a happy conclusion, and peace was once more restored.

But a worse danger had now to be encountered. For some time Burgevine had been resident at Shanghai, and rumour was busy about him. It was commonly said that he was about to join the rebels, and that he was enlisting a foreign legion from among the numerous rowdies who frequented that port. These reports and suspicions were

finally set at rest by his departure for Soochow with the
avowed purpose of co-operating with the T'aip'ings.   This
was an act of treachery of which his supporters had been
willing to think him incapable, and it created a profound
impression, not only on Li and his colleagues on the spot,
but among the highest native authorities at Peking.
Before the news reached Gordon he had attacked and
captured the towns of Kahpoo and Wukiang (Wokong),
and at the latter place had taken no fewer than 4,000
prisoners.   For the possession of these the inevitable
Ch'êng expressed a keen desire, but after the experiences
of T'aitsang Gordon thought it best to keep the chiefs
under his own control, and he could only be induced
to hand over 1,500 men to Ch'êng, and that on the condition that he should incorporate them in his own regiments.   It was not safe, however, to trust Ch'êng with the
lives of prisoners, and, to Gordon's intense disgust, he
shortly learnt that five of them had been executed.

Gordon now felt that it was fitting that some strong protest should be made against such treacherous executions.
It so happened also that at this time he had had several
passages of arms with Li on the subject of money.   In
order to put a stop to the unsoldierlike looting which had
characterised the force under Ward's command, Gordon
had desired that a gratuity should be distributed among
the troops after the capture of any place of importance.
Li, on the other hand, preferred the old and looser
system, more especially as the heavy demands made by
the war on the provincial exchequer were seriously
crippling his funds.   The system which appeared so
objectionable to Gordon was traditional to him, and he

was at a loss to understand why Gordon should object to so economical an arrangement. Frequent letters passed between them on the subject, and after the capture of Kunshan and a consequent demand for money, Li wrote agreeing to grant the sum demanded on that occasion, but giving Gordon distinctly to understand that such irregular payments were "very inconvenient." Similar financial difficulties subsequently arose with regard to the ordinary payments to be made for the expenses of the force, and Li's obstructiveness, as Gordon considered it, so irritated the commander that this, coupled with Ch'eng's treacherous conduct, determined him to resign the command. He explained his determination to Li in the following despatch :

"Your Excellency,—In consequence of the monthly difficulties I experience in getting the payment of the force made, and the non-payment of legitimate bills for boat hire and munitions of war from Her Britannic Majesty's Government, who have done so much for the Imperial Chinese Authorities, I have determined on throwing up the command of this force, as my retention of office in these circumstances is derogatory to my position as a British officer, who cannot be a suppliant for what your Excellency knows to be necessities, and which you should be only too happy to give." etc.

Acting on this determination Gordon left Kunshan for Shanghai. On his arrival at that place, however, he was met by the news of Burgevine's defection. This circumstance, he felt, completely changed the whole position. Burgevine's presence with the rebels, with the addition of the considerable body of foreign adventurers which he had carried with him, would, he felt, give a new impetus to the rebel cause. He was further aware that among the officers and men of the Ever-Victorious Army there was a strong feeling in favour of their former chief. It was remembered by them that Burgevine had lost the command by endeavouring to secure for them the pay which was their due, and it appeared not at all improbable therefore that the appearance of his standard with the T'aip'ings might result in a large desertion to the rebel ranks. In these circumstances loyalty to the cause he had adopted made Gordon forget for the moment Li's parsimony and Ch'êng's treachery, and without the loss of an hour he turned his horse's head and rode back to Kunshan. This chivalrous conduct was exactly what might have been expected from him, but it failed to elicit any expression of gratitude from Li, who seems to have been mainly concerned in making loud complaints against the American consul at Shanghai for permitting Burgevine to leave the port. How great was the danger in his eyes of Burgevine's defection may be gathered from the following despatch which he addressed to Colonel Hough, the Commandant of the British troops at Shanghai :

"The Governor has received a report through the Prefect of Sungkiang from the officer in charge of the drilled troops of that place, informing him that the Chinese steamer *Ka-Jow*, whilst on her return from this place to Sungkiang, was suddenly seized and carried off to Soochow by a large band of desperadoes. One of the men on board this steamer subsequently made his escape, and reported that he had personally seen Burgevine at the head of this band. As the man in question had heretofore been for upwards of a month residing in the same place with Burgevine, and is thoroughly well acquainted with his appearance, there is not the slightest doubt of his having accurately recognised him on this occasion.

"On receipt of this report, the Governor feels that the fact reported is really astounding. A short time ago, when it was rumoured that Burgevine had secretly visited Soochow in the interest of the rebels, and had levied a force and obtained supplies of arms and artillery for them, he at once wrote officially to the American consul, Seward, desiring him promptly to cause Burgevine's arrest, and to decide upon the proper action to be taken in his case. He next heard that Burgevine had left Shanghai at noon on the 29th July for Hu-Chow and Soochow to rejoin the rebels, and he at once sent orders to all the military stations and barriers *en route* to seize him and to send him to Shanghai. All this is on record, and while these measures are being taken, Burgevine has the audacity to head a gang of desperadoes in carrying off the *Ka-foa* steamer to Soochow. His lawlessness and rebellious designs are now patent to every eye. Should disaster hence accrue to our military movements, trade cannot be carried on in security, and thus the matter is one in which foreigners and Chinese alike cannot remain quiescent. Yet the American consul, on the receipt of the official despatch above referred to, has delayed replying with a report of the measures he has taken for arresting this man, and thus a great calamity has been fostered.

"In addition to forwarding an official communication to Mr. Consul Seward and to the French Consul-General, desiring that steps may be alike taken for the capture of Burgevine, the Governor has to communicate herewith with the honourable commandant, whom he begs to take prompt measures for causing the co-operation of the British naval and military forces with the police and Chinese troops in the field with a view to the seizure of Burgevine, and to his severe punishment in satisfaction alike of foreigners and of Chinese. He cannot be allowed to escape. This is the Governor's most earnest hope, most earnest prayer." *

* *Parliamentary Papers. China. No. 3 (1864).*

Li's alarm, so far as it was reasonable, was shared by Colonel Hough and Gordon. Both felt the importance of the crisis, and Gordon determined to move all his siege guns and ammunition to Shanghai, for fear of their being surprised at Kunshan by the now invigorated rebels. "If I had a hundred Europeans I could safely keep it where it is, but now Europeans can introduce themselves into the city, and at night might surprise our magazines," he wrote. The heavy guns he took to T'aitsang. One good was effected by the alarm. It induced Li to promise faithfully that the force should not again be in arrears of pay, and that he would at once disburse all just claims connected with it.

Sir Frederick Bruce, who had throughout supported Burgevine in opposition to Li, received the news of Burgevine's defection to the rebels with apparently mixed feelings. In the following extract from a despatch, addressed to Earl Russell, dated "Peking, September 29th, 1863," he gives some curious details of the way in which Li used his influence at Peking. "General Burgevine," writes Sir Frederick, "finding on his arrival at Shanghai that the Governor of the province refused to comply with the instructions of the Peking Government, and reinstate him in the command of Ward's force, determined on returning to Peking, to obtain a settlement of his claims on the Chinese Government.

"The Governor (*i.e.*, Li), immediately renewed, in the most offensive form, the charges by which he had originally attempted to justify his dismissal, and despatched, at the same time, the ex-superintendent of trade and General, Sieh, to support his views. This man, who has long been known for his intriguing character and retrograde views, was appointed a member of the Board of Foreign Affairs. Up to the date of his arrival at Peking, the language of His Excellency Wēnsiang to the American Minister, had been such as to lead me to hope that the charges of the Governor would be abandoned, that Burgevine's pecuniary claims would be fairly settled, and that my suggestion to find him employment at Tientsin, or some other place in China, would be adopted.

"The bad influence of Sieh's presence soon made itself felt. The charges which had been abandoned as untenable, were again brought forward, and Burgevine, despairing of justice, left for Shanghai. It was only after his departure, and by representations of the strongest character, that the Minister of the United States induced the Government to withdraw these charges. But no employment was offered to him, and Burgevine entirely failed at Shanghai in obtaining payment of the sums due as pay and for articles supplied for the use of the corps on his personal responsibility. Stung by this treatment, suffering in health from severe wounds received in the Imperial service, and ruined in his prospects, he, with a band of desperadoes of all nations, has joined the insurgents. A man who would have been a useful friend, has thus been converted into a dangerous enemy, and this result is due entirely to the injustice and perversity of the local authorities at Shanghai, to the weakness of the Central Government in allowing its orders to be disobeyed, and to that false confidence inspired in them by Major Gordon's successes, which led them to disregard suggestions which would have enabled them to remove Burgevine from the command at Shanghai, without driving him to take his last desperate step.

"Until this event happened, the Imperialists had been steadily gaining ground. Shih Ta-kai, the ablest of the T'aip'ing leaders, had been captured, and his corps broken up in Sze-chuen. The river defences of Nanking had been carried by storm, and the Chinese forces from Shanghai had driven successively the insurgents from all the positions they occupied between Shanghai and

Soochow. Though a few of the bad characters of the
coast were in the insurgent ranks, there was no leader of
repute among them, and the field open in China to the
more dangerous class of filibusters was being gradually
narrowed by the substitution in ' Ward's Corps ' of a more
reliable class as vacancies occurred.

"I cannot form an opinion as to the influence Burgevine may acquire among the Taip'ings, or the success
which may attend his efforts to organize them. The first
effect has been to reduce Major Gordon and the Chinese
troops to the defensive, and to put an end to his hopes
of the speedy capture of Soochow, which would have
given effectual security to Shanghai. I do not know
what may be Burgevine's plan of operations, but I see
there is a feeling at Shanghai that he will endeavour to
organize an expedition and strike a blow at Peking. He
could count on the support of the brigands in Shantung
and Anhui, and success at Peking would certainly overthrow the present dynasty, whether it led to the establishment of the Taip'ings or not.

"It is to be regretted that the question was looked
upon at Shanghai as one to be decided by the relative
qualifications for command of Major Gordon and Burgevine. Of the former officer I have always entertained
the highest opinion, but I fear even his abilities will not
compensate for the injury done to the Imperialist cause
by the accession of Burgevine, &c., to the insurgent ranks,
and I must further observe that the encouragement given
to the Governor, in thwarting an arrangement suggested
by the Foreign Ministers and recommended by the Central
Government, tends to weaken the central executive, which
it is our true policy to strengthen, and thereby to render
more difficult the restoration of tranquillity, and less
effectual our means of enforcing the observance of Treaties
by remonstrance at Peking, instead of by violent action at
the ports."

For some days the strain of expectation at Kunshan
was very great, but Burgevine made no sign. From
deserters Gordon learnt that he was undoubtedly at

Soochow, and that he was organising a foreign brigade in support of the rebel cause. So far as it was possible to judge, however, he took no part in the immediate warlike operations, and as therefore no new element of danger had arisen Gordon, who had for the time being thought it wise to remain on the defensive, again determined to take the field. After some heavy fighting he took Patachiao, an extensive outwork on the south face of the main stronghold. At this time it was plain that the T'aip'ings at Soochow were losing heart, and one of the first symptoms of the declining fortune of the city was an intimation received by Gordon that a number of Europeans in the rebel pay were disposed to desert to his standard. The advantage of drawing off the foreign support on which the rebels so much relied was so great that Gordon encouraged the overtures made to him by these men, and on several occasions met them on a bridge in the neighbourhood of the city to discuss their surrender. On several of these occasions Burgevine himself was present, and proposed to join the Imperialists on condition that no proceedings should be taken against him and his men for the parts they had played when in the T'aip'ing ranks. Gordon gave the necessary guarantee, but Burgevine was after all only half-hearted in his offer. The dream of empire which had filled his mind when commanding the Ever-Victorious Army still haunted his imagination, and he had the splendid audacity to propose to Gordon that they should together seize Soochow and, having organised an army of twenty thousand men, should march on Peking. It is needless to say that Gordon rejected this offer with indignant contempt. Burgevine therefore recurred to the

original proposal, and arranged with Gordon that he and
his European followers should make a sally out of the
city as though with the object of capturing the steamer
Hyson; that they should be taken on board; and that
they should be landed in the Imperial camp.

At the time appointed the sally was made, and the
Taip'ings, who advanced out of the city to support the
feigned attack, were driven back with shot and shell while
the deserters were received on board the steamer.   To
Gordon's surprise, however, Burgevine was not amongst
them, and on making enquiries he learnt that the men,
fearing that the suspicion of the rebel leaders had been
aroused, thought it best to save their own lives by making
a *sauve qui peut* without waiting to communicate with
Burgevine. With his natural chivalry Gordon at once
determined to attempt to rescue Burgevine from what he
feared was likely to be death by torture.   In pursuance of
this object he wrote to the Mu Wang, who was commanding at Soochow, asking him to allow Burgevine to
leave the city, and at the same time he returned the rifles
which the European deserters had brought with them.
It does infinite honour to the Mu Wang that he at once
complied with Gordon's request, and without let or
hindrance Burgevine was allowed to follow his companions
to the Imperialists' camp.   This conduct of the rebel
leader compares favourably with the action of the
Imperialists under Li at the final surrender of the city,
and it is much to be doubted whether such a request from
the opposite camp would have been granted by the
Governor under similar circumstances.

Disaffection, of which the desertion of the foreigners

was the first symptom, now made rapid strides in
Soochow, and after the capture of several outworks, where
the rebels fought well under the direct command of Mu
Wang, it was intimated to Gordon through General Ch'êng
that, with the exception of this leader, all the Wangs in
Soochow, with the expectant princes and thirty thousand
men, were anxious to join the Imperial ranks. In the
communications that passed with these men a proposal
was made that Gordon should attack the stockades outside the East Gate, and that when Mu Wang with his
wonted courage should lead the sally for the protection of
the outworks, they should shut the gate behind him, and
then surrender the city in due form. It was impossible
that negotiations which were known to so many people
should be carried on without some suspicion being aroused
in the mind of Mu Wang. From various indications he
gathered that some such plot was afoot, and he determined
to face the difficulty at once. With this object he
summoned the Wangs to a conference, when, after having
dined and prayed, a state conclave was held, at which all
the Kings appeared in their robes and crowns. No
record of the discussion exists, but from all accounts it
rapidly became animated and heated. But it was short,
for at the moment when the debate was at its height one
of the Kings drew his dagger and stabbed Mu Wang
to death. The murder was a foul one, and was speedily
to be avenged. Events further proved that, like so many
deeds of political violence, it was superfluous, for from
evidence acquired later Gordon learnt that the Mu Wang
had been anxiously trying to communicate with him for
several days with a view to surrender.

The city was now virtually given up, and Gordon, who had arranged with Li that he should receive the submission of the Wangs, to whom he agreed to show mercy as a condition of their surrender, made preparations for marching his force out of the reach of the temptations offered by loot, to attack Woosich and Changchow Foo. He knew well, however, that his officers and men would justly be dissatisfied if they received no reward for the hard work and strenuous fighting they had gone through before the surrender, and he therefore asked Li, who had come from Shanghai to take part in the final capitulation of the town, to grant the men a gratuity of two months' pay. This Li declined to do, and in reply Gordon informed him that he would give him until three o'clock on the same day to consider the matter, and if at that hour he should still be of the same mind that he (Gordon) would feel bound to resign his command. Before the appointed time General Ch'eng appeared to offer terms, and begged Gordon to compromise the affair by accepting for his men one month's pay. As time pressed Gordon addressed his men, and urged them to accept the money. At first the troops were inclined to be mutinous, and threatened to march down and take possession of the Governor's person. Gordon's influence, however, was sufficient to prevent this extreme measure, and the disturbance was ultimately quelled, though Gordon thought it prudent to leave a guard on the Governor's boat, lest violence should be done him before the troops marched off. How infamously Gordon's consideration for Li was rewarded is best told in Gordon's own words. In a " Memorandum on the events occurring between the 28th November and

6th December, 1863, inclusive," he writes as follows on the tragedy which was perpetrated on the day succeeding his discussion with Li on the subject of the gratuity. After mentioning that he had gone into Soochow he adds :

"I then went into the city, to Lar-Wang's house, reaching it at 11.30 o'clock a.m. I had heard that the Wangs had to go out to the Fut'ai at 12 o'clock noon, and that then the city would be given over. I should mention that General Ch'êng had told me on the afternoon of the 5th December that the Fut'ai had written to Pekin respecting the capture of Soochow, and stating that he had amnestied the prisoners. At the Lar-Wang's house I met all the Wangs, with their horses saddled, to leave for the Fut'ai. I took Lar-Wang aside, and asked him if everything was all right. He said 'Yes.' I then told him I had the intention of going to the Taho Lake to look for the *Firefly*. He said he was coming down to see me, and would like me to stop two or three days. I said unless he thought there was an absolute necessity, the business I was going on was too important for me to stop ; but that if he thought he had any reason for wishing me to stay, I would do so. He said 'No,' and I bade him and the other Wangs good-bye, and they all passed me a few minutes afterwards with twenty (20) attendants going towards the Low-mün, or East Gate, on their way to the Fut'ai.

"I went down to Mo-Wang's palace, and saw General Ch'êng's men come down to bury Mo-Wang's body according to my request. I then went on to the East Gate, or Low-mün, to wile away the time until the steamers got round to Wuhlungchow, intending to go round the wall to the Pou-mün, or South Gate. Just as we arrived at the gate I saw a large crowd on the bank opposite the Fut'ai's boat, and soon afterwards a large force of Imperialists came into the city and ran off to the right and left along the wall and into the city, yelling, as they usually do when they enter a vacated stockade, and firing off

their muskets in the air. I remonstrated with the
mandarins and soldiers, as their conduct was liable to
frighten the rebels, who might retaliate and cause a
row. After a few minutes General Ch'êng came in, and
I noticed he looked disturbed. I asked him eagerly if
the interview was over and had been satisfactory. He
said the Wangs had never come to the Fut'ai. I said
I had seen them going, and asked him what could have
become of them. He said he did not know, but thought
they might have run away. I asked him what could have
induced them to do so. He said they had sent out to the
Fut'ai to ask to keep twenty thousand (20,000) men, and
to have half of the city, building a wall inside—that
Lar-Wang had said before that he wanted only two
thousand five hundred (2,500), and that at another
time he said he wanted no soldiers but merely to
retire home — that the Fut'ai had objected to his
demand, and that he had told him to go to the
Teh-mün, and stockade his men outside that gate,
and that he supposed Lar-Wang had taken alarm and
gone off. He said further that Lar-Wang had sent to
Chung-Wang for assistance. I asked him if he thought
Lar-Wang and the other Wangs had gone back to the
rebels. He said no, but they would go back to their own
homes and live there. I did not feel very well satisfied,
and asked Mr. Macartney, who was by, to go to
Lar-Wang's house and see if he was there, and to re-
assure him if he was alarmed at anything. General Ch'êng
was anxious I should not go, and as I had no suspicion, I
went round the wall with him to the Pou-mün, which we
reached at five o'clock p.m. I had frequently returned to
the question of Lar-Wang, but found that both General
Ch'êng and my interpreter seemed to evade the questions.
When I got to the Pou-mün I told General Ch'êng I
should go no further, as I felt uncomfortable about
Lar-Wang, and also heard volleys of musketry in the
city, but not of any great amount. I asked General
Ch'êng what it was. He said there were some Kwangsi
and Canton men who would not shave, and they were
driving them out of the city, having left two gates open for

their retreat, but they were only frightening them out. General Ch'êng then left, and I asked my interpreter what he thought of the state of affairs. He said that he thought the Imperialists, having got the city, did not care about keeping their agreement. I therefore decided on riding to Lar-Wang's house and seeing him if possible. I rode with my interpreter through the streets, which were full of rebels standing to their arms, and Imperialist soldiers looting. I went to Lar-Wang's palace, and found it ransacked. I met Lar-Wang's uncle, a second in command, and he begged me to come to his house and protect it. He then withdrew the female household of Lar-Wang and accompanied them to his house, where there were some thousand (1,000) rebels under arms in a barricaded street. It was now dark, and having seen the state of affairs, I wished much that Lar-Wang's uncle would let my interpreter go, taking orders for the steamers to come round and take the Fut'ai prisoner (as he, the interpreter, thought that the Fut'ai had not yet beheaded the Wangs), and also an order to bring up my force. They unfortunately would not let my interpreter go, and I remained with them until two o'clock a.m. on the 7th, when I persuaded them to let him go and procure assistance. I had kept several bands from looting the house by my presence. About 3 a.m. one of the men who had gone out with the interpreter returned, and said that a body of Imperialists had seized the interpreter and wounded him. I was now apprehensive of a general massacre, as the man made me understand that the order I had sent had been torn up, and therefore went out to go to the Pou-mün to send by my boat additional orders, and also to look for the interpreter. I found no traces of him, and proceeding to the Pou-mün was detained an hour by the Imperialists. It was then 5 a.m., and I determined on proceeding for my guard to the Low-mün, or East Gate, hoping to be able to seize the Fut'ai, and to get back in time to save the house of Lar-Wang's uncle.

"I got to the Low-mün at 6 a.m., and sent on my guard to the house. It was, however, too late : it had been ransacked. I then left the city and met General Ch'êng at the gate. I told him what I thought, and then proceeded to the stockade to await the steamers. As I was still ignorant that the Wangs had been beheaded, I thought that they were prisoners, and might still be rescued if the Fut'ai could be secured. When awaiting the steamers, General Ch'êng sent down Major Bailey—one of the officers I had sent him to command his artillery— who told me that General Ch'êng had gone into the city, and sat down and cried. He then, to alleviate his grief, shot down twenty of his men for looting, and sent Major Bailey to tell me he had nothing to do with the matter, that the Fut'ai ordered him to do what he did, and that the Fut'ai had ordered the city to be looted. I asked Major Bailey if the Wangs had been beheaded. He said that he had heard so. He then told me he had Lar-Wang's son in his boat, and had brought him to me. The son came up, and pointing to the other side, said that his father and the Wangs had been beheaded there. I went over and found six bodies, and recognised Lar-Wang's head. The hands and bodies were gashed in a frightful way, and cut down the middle. Lar-Wang's body was partially buried." *

Gordon's grief and anger at this inhuman treachery were unbounded. He felt that his honour as a British officer had been outraged, and his sense of humanity was shocked at so foul a murder. For himself he cared nothing, but it was the wrong done to the British uniform he wore which tried him to the utmost. He recognised also the folly of the crime, for he was firmly persuaded that if these Wangs had met with honourable treatment, the commanders in other towns would have been prepared to surrender. On Li the whole weight of his condemnation rested, and in the first moment of rage he, for the first time during the campaign, took a weapon into his

* *Parliamentary Papers. China.* No. 3 (1864).

hand. Armed with a rifle, he went to Li's boat, determined to execute summary punishment upon the malefactor. General Ch'êng, however, had seen enough of Gordon's state of mind when his suspicions had been first aroused with regard to the fate of the Wangs to know that danger threatened, and he hurried off to Li to warn him that evil was intended against him. Li took the hint with an alacrity which showed that however little value he put on other men's lives he thought a good deal of his own. With all speed he left his boat and fled into the city, where he succeeded in hiding himself, although Gordon sought him day and night. Finding that his intended victim had escaped from his hands, Gordon withdrew his force to Kunshan, and wrote to Li an indignant letter, in which, while proclaiming the infamy of his conduct, he resigned the command of the force. At the same time he wrote to General Brown, communicating to him his determination, and giving in full the reasons which had induced him to take this course.

General Brown cordially approved of Gordon's action, and went up to Kunshan to relieve him from the command. Li was still at Soochow, and General Brown determined to see him in order to express plainly his views on his conduct. At this time Li, who was thoroughly alarmed, was anxious to make his peace, and, like all Chinamen under similar circumstances, he after having repeatedly treated the General with studied discourtesy, was now profuse in his civilities, and instead of awaiting the General's arrival within the walls of the city, went out a considerable distance to greet him. Li was evidently ill at ease during the interview, but declined to acknowledge that he had done anything wrong; at the same time he readily agreed to make a public declaration, exonerating Gordon from all share in the massacre. He also assented to the General's determination that the Ever-Victorious Army should remain inactive, pending the decision of the Peking authorities on the massacre. He expressed great relief on hearing that Gordon had consented to remain in temporary command, but the General emphatically warned him, that on the recurrence of any such treachery he should immediately withdraw all the British officers serving with the Imperialists. The conduct of Li throughout the whole siege of Soochow was thoroughly characteristic of his countrymen. When Burgevine joined the rebels with his ragged regiment of foreign rowdies, Li's alarm was almost craven. He implored General Brown to assist him in the capture of the new allies to the rebel cause. He wrote to the American Consul begging him to seize Burgevine, he urged Gordon to use every endeavour to arrest him, and he offered 10,000 taels to anyone who would bring him a prisoner to his camp. But Burgevine and his followers had no sooner surrendered to the Imperialists than he entirely changed his tone, and professed to consider it a matter of complete indifference whether they were with the rebels or not. In the same spirit his terror was great for some days after the surrender of the city, and so long as it was doubtful whether or not Gordon would remain with the force. But the instant that important point was settled he resumed his old cavalier treatment of the Army, and pretended to regard its services as of minor importance to the Imperial cause.

Captain Sherard Osborn, of whom mention will presently be made, may possibly be accused of having held prejudiced views regarding Li's character, but in a memorandum he wrote with reference to the Governor's conduct towards himself and Gordon, he succeeded in giving accurate expression to the very general opinion which was held by foreigners on the spot of Li's behaviour.

"Futai Li," he wrote, "is an able Chinaman, and as unprincipled as all Chinese officials. His plan would be to render me powerless, and then to use or toss me aside just as he does all European leaders in his force. He is a civilian by education, ruling over military and naval affairs without the slightest knowledge of either. . . . Having secured the services of an excellent officer in Major Gordon, who appears to have entered his service, not that of the Emperor of China, . . . Futai Li proceeds to render him powerless, and to hamper his action in two ways; first by depriving him of the means to carry out any decisive measures, and next by placing in exactly similar positions a number of other Europeans, and playing one off against the other. Major Gordon wishes to attack Soochow Foo, and asks for one hundred Europeans. The Futai agrees, but says the hundred men must only be entered for one month. Gordon declines to enter into any such agreement, seeing its injustice and folly. The Futai insults him by questioning his desire to fight the rebels, and proposes that the assaulting column should be formed of all European officers in his employ, and that over their bodies the Chinese would advance to victory.

"Again, what faith can I have in any Mandarin's listening to my advice as a subordinate, when I am told by General Brown, commander-in-chief of our military forces in China, and the superior of the Futai, that he will listen to no advice or suggestion the general offers, and that he purposely avoids all conference with him; and when an interview is sought by General Brown, insolently replies that he is too busy to see him." *

* *Parliamentary Papers. China. No. 2 (1864).*

The opinions thus expressed were shared to a certain extent by Sir Frederick Bruce, who expressed his view that the murder of the Wangs was an "atrocious massacre," and that it would be quite impossible to expect any British officer of character to serve under the orders of, or with, Governor Li if such proceedings were to be tolerated for an instant. Pending the reference to Peking, Gordon's force remained inactive. Not so Li, who was using every effort to gain the support and approval of the Emperor and his advisers. The death of the Wangs precluded the possibility of gaining any direct evidence from their side of the question. But according to Mr. Interpreter Mayers, who made a careful investigation of the subject, it appears that the chiefs on reaching the camp were received with friendly demonstrations by Li, who congratulated them on joining the Imperial forces, and mentioned the buttons which, as emblems of their future ranks, they were to receive. He then handed them over to General Ch'êng, who kept them in friendly talk until the executioners rushed upon the scene and beheaded them. This version is thoroughly in keeping with the Chinese mode of procedure, and bears on the face of it the resemblance of truth. Li, however, had a different tale to tell. In his despatch to the Tsungli Yamên he stated that instead of coming as repentant rebels pleading for mercy, the Wangs had entered his presence with unshaven heads, wearing their arms, and with all the appearance of "extreme ferocity." That they had demanded the right to command their own men, to hold a certain portion of the city, and that high rank should be given them; and that they had threatened that if these conditions were not fulfilled they would return to the rebel camp. In these circumstances the Governor declared that he felt it incumbent on him to execute them to encourage the others, and he claimed that the result was eminently salutary, inasmuch that the remaining officers and men at once shaved their heads, and adopted the pigtail style of headdress peculiar to the present dynasty. It is almost unnecessary to say that Li's version of the story was readily accepted by the Emperor, who, on the receipt of the full report of the surrender of Soochow, issued the following edict :

" Li Hungchang (Governor of Kiangsu) reports that the army under his command has captured the city Soochow, and exterminated (the rebels within its walls). The rebels had been reduced to great extremity ; and those of them who were desirous of returning to their allegiance, together with the Imperial troops, entered the city, destroyed the rebel army, and so recaptured the province of Kiangsu.

"The reading of this report has afforded His Majesty sincere delight and gratification.

"Soochow, the capital of the Province of Kiangsu, was four years ago captured by the rebels, and has remained in their hands ever since. The army, acting under orders from Li Hungchang, captured in succession the lines of rebel works outside the four gates of the city, and so struck terror into the enemy in the city that urgent offers of returning to allegiance were made.

"On the 30th of November the Chung Wang, seeing that the attacks of the Imperial troops were daily becoming more vigorous, and that the rebels in the city were in a state of disorganization, fled under cover of night with more than 10,000 of his death-deserving adherents; handing over the city to the old rebel, Mu Wang (Fan Shao Kuang), with orders to defend it to the death.

"On the 3rd and 4th of December the naval and military forces under Ch'êng-Hsio-ch'i, Li Ch'ou-pin and

Huang Yi-shêng attacked the different gates of the city, keeping up day and night an incessant assault, which became more vigorous the longer it lasted. Gordon also established himself close to the city walls, and opened a cannonade against them.

"On the 4th December the Mu Wang (Mo Wang) ascended the walls to direct the defence ; when at the head of his men and in the act of issuing orders, a rebel leader named Kao Ying-Kuan, who with others had entered into a conspiracy with a rebel officer named Wang Yü-Wei against him, took him off his guard and stabbed him to death. After killing more than a thousand of Mu Wang's associates, they threw open the gates and came out to give in their allegiance. Ch'êng-Hsio-ch'i with the troops under his command entered the city, and having posted his soldiers, searched out and killed above a thousand of the surviving rebels. Li Ch'ou-pin attacked and killed great numbers who were escaping by the Pan Mén, and set at liberty several thousands of prisoners.

"The recapture of the provincial capital was thus effected.

" His Majesty directs Li Hungchang to take advantage of this victory to march with his troops upon Changchow, which city having been captured, he will join his forces with those before Nanking, sweep that place clear of rebels (*lit.*, sweep the dens and take possession of the pools), and free the river of their presence.

" His Majesty commands the Board of War to confer suitable honours on Tsêng Kwofan, Minister of State and Governor-General of the two Kiang, who sent a contingent to assist in the recapture of this noted city.

" Li Hungchang, since he entered office as Governor of Kiangsu, has displayed great prudence and calculation, and his skilful tactics have been completely successful ; he has again and again captured cities and gained honours on the field of battle ; and now the recapture of Soochow by his troops renders him still more worthy of praise. As a mark of his sincere approbation, His Majesty is pleased o confer upon him the honorary title of 'Guardian of the Heir-Apparent,' and to present him with a yellow jacket.

'Huang I-Shêng and Li Ch'ou-pin, in addition to receiving the hereditary rank of Yün ch'i Yu (a title with fourth rank button attached), are recommended to the notice of the Board of War. Ch'êng Hsio-ch'i receives the same rank as the above, and in addition is presented with a yellow jacket.

"Gordon, specially appointed a General in the army of Kiangsu, was in command of troops who assisted in these operations; His Majesty, in order to evince his approval of the profound skill and great zeal displayed by him, orders him to receive a military decoration of the first rank and a sum of 10,000 taels." *

(Here follows a list of honours and rewards conferred upon officers engaged.)

It will be seen from this despatch that either Li was strangely misinformed, or that he had grossly misrepresented the facts. His account of the murder of Mu Wang is a complete travestie of the truth, and his account of the part which he played in the operations against the city are curiously self-laudatory, while the very subordinate part which he assigns to Gordon presents a strange picture of combined ingratitude and inaccuracy. A day or two later (14th December, 1863) a further decree commendatory of Gordon was issued, which ran as follows:

"Li is enjoined to communicate Our decree of approval and praise to Gordon for the great bravery and exertions which attended the recapture of Soochow. The donation of ten thousand taels is to be provided and sent to him by Li. Foreign nations already possess orders of merit under the name of stars. Let, therefore, the decoration of the first class which We have conferred upon Gordon be arranged in accordance with this system. Respect this."

* *Parliamentary Papers. China.* No. 7 (1864).

In obedience to this decree Li sent messengers bearing the Imperial presents to the still incensed Gordon, and probably never before in the history of the Empire have Imperial messengers bearing gifts been so received as these men were on this occasion. They entered Gordon's presence with all the pomp and circumstance which commonly surround Imperial benefactions. But Gordon was in no humour to receive money and gifts tainted with blood, and he was no sooner made aware of the object of the visit of the messengers than taking in his hand the well-known wand with which he had so often led his troops to victory, he belaboured the emissaries soundly, and drove them with their presents from his house. Only those who know the almost sacred value attaching to presents conferred by Eastern potentates can imagine the stupefaction of the messengers and the surprise of Li. That a man should decline honours was within the mental grasp of the Governor, but that he should refuse to receive ten thousand taels passed his comprehension.

It is customary for Mandarins, and Li is no exception to the rule, to regard all foreigners of being greedy only of gain. The trading relations of the Western Powers with China have so vastly overshadowed every other interest that there is some excuse for this misapprehension which naturally finds ready acceptance with Chinese officials, among whom an act of financial disinterestedness is almost unknown. Gordon's rejection, therefore, of the Emperor's ten thousand taels was a matter of surprise to many. But it opened Li's eyes to the chivalrous character of the man, and thus laid the foundation for that esteem and respect with which he regarded him in after years.

Although Li's account of the murder of the Wangs was amply sufficient to justify him in the eyes of the Emperor and his advisers, Gordon and his supporters continued to maintain an irreconcileable attitude towards him. Sir Frederick Bruce spoke both and wrote to Prince Kung in the strongest terms on the subject of the "atrocious massacre," as he styled it, and gave the Prince plainly to understand that no British officer of character would serve under the orders of, or with, Governor Li until the matter had been fully investigated and explained. In the opinion of the Prince all this was much ado about nothing, and he refused to admit more than that Li had made a mistake, in not having at once explained to Gordon the necessity which had induced him to behead the Wangs.

Meanwhile Li was becoming restive at Gordon's inactivity, which was, unquestionably, beginning to produce unfortunate results. As matters stood large sums were being expended on the force, in return for which Li was receiving nothing. It was said, and with apparent reason, that his impatience had tempted him to tamper with some of the officers and to hint to them his determination to dismiss Gordon if he continued to refuse to take the field. The effect of this manœuvring soon became apparent on Gordon's officers, who in times of peace were always troublesome and unruly, and who now showed manifest signs of insubordination. To such lengths did this mutinous spirit go that Gordon was compelled to dismiss from the force sixteen of the malcontents before the spirit of disorder was laid. Another disturbing cause was the presence of Burgevine at Shanghai. This

adventurer had, as it was well known, been enlisting
Europeans for a secret service, and information which
reached Gordon left no doubt in his mind that the secret
service was service in the rebel ranks. All these causes,
added to the softening influence of time, induced Gordon
to reconsider his position. Li's friends had daily poured
into his ears plausible accounts of the Governor's difficulties and conduct, and by degrees he began to look with
less anger on the massacre of the Wangs, as well as to
recognise the serious evils which he was entailing on
the country by the inactivity of the force. At this time it
happened that a most powerful advocate of Li's views
arrived at Shanghai. Mr. Hart, now Sir Robert Hart,
who had succeeded Mr. Lay in the direction of the
Chinese customs, having come to that port on official
business, paid a visit to Major Gordon to consult with
him on matters connected with the rebellion. Mr. Hart
had, in his opinion, sufficient evidence to justify him in
considering that Gordon took an unduly harsh view of
Li's conduct, and the result of the exposition of Mr.
Hart's views was that an interview was arranged between the high contending parties. At this meeting a
complete reconciliation took place, and Gordon agreed
to take the field at once, on condition that Li should
issue the following proclamation explanatory of his conduct and exonerating Gordon from all share in the
treachery :

"The Ever-Victorious Force, since the command was
taken by General Gordon, has assisted with uniform
success, in the operations against the rebels, and the
Fut'ai has on repeated occasions obtained decrees of
approbation for its services in reply to his memorials to

the Throne. At the time when the rebel Kao, falsely known as Na Wang, and his associates were summarily put to death, the overthrow of settled arrangements was imminent from one moment to another, and General Gordon, not being on the spot, could not be cognizant of the circumstances involved. He was thus led to conceive that the course of action adopted was in opposition to the agreement previously entered into ; and now, as both Chinese and foreigners appear to attach credence to mere rumours, and are ignorant that the Futai's intentions, although seemingly at variance with those of General Gordon, were in fact identical with them, it behoves him to remove all doubt upon this subject by the issue of one distinct Proclamation.

" The facts to be stated are these :

" At the moment when the operations against Soo-chow were on the point of being crowned with success, the rebel Kao and his associates, finding themselves in straits, besought permission to surrender. A great distinction existed between this act and the submission tendered before the arrival of a besieging force, by the rebel garrisons of Na-wei, Chang-shu, and other places. When General Gordon obtained the Fut'ai's consent to admit them to surrender, in order to avert the slaughter that must have ensued upon the storming of the city, it was from a desire to spare the myriads of the population, and not simply with the wish at all hazards to secure the lives of the rebel Kao and his associates. Still less can it be said that when once the agreement was entered into, no alteration was possible, so that these men could have been empowered, in tendering their submission, to en-force claims on their own behalf, and in despite of all, be still held as pardoned, whilst their rebellious ten-dencies were arising afresh ! This principle is perfectly clear, and both the law of China and foreign practice are identical upon this point, respecting which there can be no doubt.

" At first, in the negotiations for the submission for the murder of the so styled Mu Wang, the surrender of the North-east gate, and the fixing of a time for their inter-

view at the camp, every step was known to General
Gordon ; but on his arrival at the camp, the so styled Na
Wang had not shaved his head, and his rebellious designs
were patent to view.   He both refused to disband his
men, and insisted on their being enrolled in the army, to
the number of several tens of battalions, and further urged
the demand that the ranks of Brigadier-General, &c.,
should be obtained from the Throne for his adherents,
who were to be left at the head of their men as garrison
for Soochow.   Not only was no sign of contrition
evinced, but, on the contrary, there was a design of
preparing the way for an eventual return to rebellion.
Whilst his speech was evasive and ambiguous, his
expression of countenance was ferocious and bold to an
extreme ; and all this took place after the surrender had
been completed.   The Fut'ai could, therefore, for his own
safety, do no otherwise than guard against a (dangerous)
departure from the arranged conditions ; and these were
all particulars with which General Gordon was not acquainted.   As regards the outset, when the Fut'ai agreed
with General Gordon to accept the submission of these
men, he had no conception that hesitation would take
place at the last moment ; and with respect to subsequent
occurrences, the signs of danger were disclosed in a single
instant, when, if no action could have been taken until
after communicating with General Gordon, not only would
it have become too late, but all the advantages secured
would have been sacrificed.   Supposing that the Fut'ai
had adhered rigidly (to his agreement), so that these few
bandits had been enabled to ensure their own safety and
resort to their rebellious practices, it would have been
many tens of thousands who would have suffered by the
consequent misfortune ; and the result would have been
far from what was contemplated when first these men
were admitted to surrender.   Fortunately, however, by a
summary decision at the vital instant, by which these few
bandits only were put to death, and the mass of their
followers scattered to the winds, benefit was secured to
the same vast number of the people, whom to protect
was the main object held in view.

"From first to last what was aimed at was the prevention of slaughter in the moment of victory at Soochow; and therefore has the Fut'ai said that his intentions, though seemingly at variance, were in reality identical with those of Major Gordon. When, in fact, on the 6th of December, the so-styled Na Wang came with his associates to the camp, General Gordon, having previously looked upon the matter as securely settled, did not accompany them; and, after the occurrence, he returned to Quin-san. He was thus both not an eye-witness to what actually occurred on the spot, and he was misled by the rumours which were spread abroad after the affair had taken place. He was impressed with the conviction that, the terms of surrender having been agreed to, the subsequent execution of the individuals was a breach of the Convention entered into; but he was totally unaware of the pressing urgency and extreme danger of the consequences involved, which left not an instant for delay, and which led the Fut'ai to inflict at once the penalty prescribed by military law.

"The Fut'ai has already written a minute account of these circumstances to the Board of Foreign Affairs for communication to the Foreign Ministers; and, in addition to this, he now publishes this Proclamation for the information of Chinese and foreigners alike.

"He will take stringent measures to prohibit the circulation of false and inflammatory reports.

"Tung-Chih, *3rd year*, 1st moon, *7th day*
"(*February* 14, 1864)." *

---

* *Parliamentary Papers. China.* No. 7 (1864).

WITH the appearance of this proclamation the feud came to an end, and Gordon once more took the field. To both men this renewed activity was a matter for congratulation. Gordon had seen enough of the miseries incurred by the presence of the T'aip'ings to desire in the cause of humanity to rescue the survivors from like distress. He had seen whole districts laid waste; he had seen villages destroyed; and he had seen everything in the shape of provisions snatched from the hungry grasp of the inhabitants. He had seen people die, by hundreds, of starvation, and, worst of all, he had seen only too evident traces in the mangled corpses which encumbered the ground that want had driven the wretched people to cannibalism. To Li these things were of little moment. His one absorbing idea was the suppression of the rebellion, which was still threatening and aggressive. Like all Chinamen in the presence of difficulties, he was cordial and polite to the man to whom he looked to save him from his enemies. Things worked smoothly therefore for a time. All arrears due

to Gordon's men were punctually paid up, and matters
between the two chiefs went like a marriage bell.

Gordon's plan of campaign was to cut the rebel forces
in two by marching on Yesing and Liyang, and thus
to open communications with Tsêng Kwofan before
Nanking. With ease he captured the first-named city,
and fulfilled the concluding part of his programme by
accepting the surrender of Liyang. In a further expedition against Kintang, however, he was not only unsuccessful in the assault on the city, but was wounded
in the attack. To add to his difficulties he at the same
time received a special message from Li imploring him
to come to Changchow Fu to assist in the attack on that
place. At the head of three thousand men he was
carried, for he was unable to walk, to the assistance of
the Governor. Li had confidently expected that the city
would have fallen, and he expressed his indignation in no
measured terms at the inactivity of his native generals.

At this crisis his dependence on Gordon became
greater, owing to the very serious loss he sustained in
the death of General Ch'êng.

Li's attitude at this time was a curious illustration of
his dependence on Gordon, and of his jealousy of the
Ever-Victorious Army. He was anxious to have him
at hand to advise and support him in case of emergency,
but he was at the same time desirous above all things
to have the entire glory of capturing the town. Changchow had been originally taken by the rebels on the 11th
May, 1860, and Li determined to attack the city on the
anniversary of that event. In the first assault, undertaken independently of Gordon, Li's troops were driven

back discomfited, and the same result would have attended the second onslaught if Gordon had not led up two of his regiments to support Li's men, who were already flying from the breaches. With the fall of this town the suppression of the rebellion in the province of Kiangsu was practically complete. It was fortunate for Li that this was so, for besides having at this time to lament the loss of General Ch'eng, who had been killed in an attack on Kashing Fu, he had to submit to the withdrawal of the Order in Council which had authorised Gordon to accept service under the Chinese Government. Ch'eng, who had begun his military career as a rebel, had since his return to the Imperial ranks fought well and ably under Li's orders. He had shown considerable strategic power, and had gained the full confidence of his men.

That Gordon had complaints to make against him for cruelty and shiftiness, is only tantamount to saying that he was a Chinaman.

His loss to the Imperial cause was doubtless very great, and in the following memorial presented to the Emperor by Li, which is quoted in Wilson's *Ever-Victorious Army*, the Governor expresses, in the quaint language common to his countrymen, his appreciation of his merits:

"Ch'eng, the Tsung-Ping of Nanchang, was formally presented with the hereditary rank of Shao-pei (Yun chi Wei). He was subsequently made Patulu (a Manchu distinction). Fiercely he attacked the city of Kashing. where he was wounded in the head by a ball which pierced his brain. He fainted, but was afterwards restored to consciousness, and borne back (to Soochow) to be put under medical treatment. He himself knew that his wound was desperate, but he refused to take medicine. I over and over again exhorted him to submit to treatment, and I called in doctors who professed to cure both internal and external maladies, so that he at last consented to put himself in their hands. His mind and speech then soon became clear. I left Soochow on the 7th April for the purpose of following up the Rebels, but at the moment of starting I visited him. He said that although the Rebels had been defeated, their strength was still not to be despised, and he told me to order the officers to be careful in battle. He also remarked that brave men were not easily obtained, and bitterly regretted his own fate, by which he was prevented from following up his duty to the country in exterminating the Rebels. He sobbed and sighed, and tears came into his eyes while he was speaking to me. I, on the other hand, bade him be of good courage, and told him that he would thus hasten his recovery, and that it was not necessary for him to grieve and be anxious. When I departed I left directions that the local Mandarins should visit him from time to time. While I was at Kongyin attacking the Rebels there, a report suddenly reached me that Ch'êng was gradually sinking. His senses had not, however, deserted him. On the 14th April he called his servant, and ordered him to bring the Yellow Jacket presented to him by your Majesty, and assist him to put it on. He then bowed his head towards your Majesty's palace, and walked round his room. Seeing tea on the table, he took up a cupful and attempted to drink, but the fluid could not pass down his throat. By this he was much moved, and wept. He ordered Han Chu, a Chichao who had the superintendence of the camp, to mount a horse and come to me to beg that I would carefully follow out my design of destroying the Rebels. He further said that he knew he could not see me again in the provincial city. There was not a particle of selfishness in his recommendations. At the time when he felt death approaching, he bemoaned the unfinished state of the work he had cut out for himself. He felt that he had not returned the favours heaped on him by your Majesty. The fluid of his brain continued to run out of the wound, and on the 15th April, at twelve o'clock at night, he died. I was excessively grieved. All the military officers cried bitterly. Every one, whether belonging to Kiangsu or to Chekiang, whether Mandarins or scholars or common people, lamented his death.

"I then examined into Ch'êng's previous history, and I discovered that he came from T"ungch'ênghien, in the province of Nganhwui, whence, during the Rebel troubles, he was taken as a prisoner. The Four-Eyed Dog, Ying, placed great confidence in him. Ch'êng, because he saw that the Rebels oppressed the people, at length made an attempt to get away from them. The Rebels, however, managed to secure him again, and shut him up so that he could not escape. In the fourth month of the eleventh year of the Emperor, whose style was Hien-fung, Tseng Kwo-tsun, the Futai of Chekiang, led his soldiers to Nganking. Ch'êng, without mentioning the affair to anybody, came over to the camp occupied by Tseng Chun-kan (Tseng Kwo-tsun's brother) and surrendered himself. He was instantly recognised as a superior man, and one far above the general run of Rebel officers who had joined the camp, and was sent with the expedition which recovered Nganking, where his bravery was most conspicuous. The Governor-General, Tseng Kwo-fan, reported the affair to your Majesty, and pledged himself for Ch'êng's work. At the same time I myself was at Nganking, and constantly heard of Ch'êng's exploits, as well as of his wisdom, daring, and varied ability. Shortly afterwards, when your Majesty ordered me to hurry to Shanghai, I begged Tseng Kwo-fan to allow me to carry with me Ch'êng's two camps . . .

"When Soochow fell, Kow Yeuen-kuan (who was the chief man among the Rebel Wangs who submitted to us), with eight others, proposed to divide the city into two parts. At this time these fellows had about 200,000 men under their command, and they thought that they could altogether neutralise any effort we might make. If this demand had been granted, and if, subsequently, the slightest opposition had been made to their wishes, they

would have had 'my head in chancery' in no time.
But Ch'êng told me that as he had formerly been among
the Rebels, he well knew their mode of thought, and that
as their crimes had been outrageous, their punishment
ought to be proportionately severe. 'Cut off,' said he,
'the heads of their leaders, and their myriads of followers
will instantly subside into insignificance. You will thus
secure the tranquillity of the city.' I therefore immediately ordered the execution of the Wangs, and restored
tranquillity to their followers. Thus were the mighty
difficulties which at first presented themselves at once
solved. He was able to calculate beforehand, and he
was also able to act with decision. Among the leaders of
modern times there were few like him. When Gordon
heard of his death he wept and groaned. He had seen
with his own eyes how excellent he was as a general.
Indeed, so highly did Gordon value him that he begged
me to give him as a keepsake the two banners which
Ch'êng used to carry into battle, that he might bear them
to his own country, and thus preserve the memory of one
he loved so well. Ch'êng possessed a mind of no ordinary
depth and capacity. His plans and their subsequent
execution were most clearly and minutely considered.
His own countrymen and foreigners alike admired him ;
and had heaven vouchsafed to him many years of life,
it would have been seen that his labours were not finished
at the period of his actual death . . .

"Now, since it was in the service of the country that he
lost his life, is it not right that I should beg your Majesty
to manifest your favour towards him in the manner due to
a Ti-Tu who dies on the field of battle? I also beg your
Majesty to give him a posthumous rank, and to cause the
story of his life to be inscribed on the records of this
dynasty. Moreover I would suggest that at Nganking Fu,
Soochow Fu, Kashing Fu, commemorative temples be
raised to his exclusive honour, so as to celebrate his
faithfulness. If your Majesty be pleased to do this,
it will be a proof of your extraordinary favour.

"I would further inform your Majesty that at the time
of writing the above despatch I received the Imperial

F

edict, dated the 4th April, relative to the gifts to be presented to Ch'èng, on account of the conquest of Kashing, viz., a white jade feather ornament, a white jade thumb-ring, a jade-handled knife, and a pair of pouches. I reverently ordered these presents to be carried to Soochow, and presented to Ch'èng's family, to be placed before his coffin to solace his noble soul."

In other circumstances the dissolution of the Ever-Victorious Army, which was a necessary consequence of Gordon's resignation, would have been a still further blow to the Imperial cause. But now that Nanking was practically the only city holding out against the Imperialists, Li felt himself quite able to cope with the smouldering embers of disaffection which might remain, and it was evidently with some feeling of relief that he contemplated the disbandment of the force. The matter was not quite so simple as at first sight appeared. Li was well aware that Gordon's officers, though brave and skilful, were after all soldiers of fortune, and that it was always possible that, if suddenly sent about their business, they might join the rebels, and revive again the T'aip'ing movement. He therefore consulted Gordon, who recommended that the officers and men should be given gratuities, according to their ranks and services, and should be furnished with means, in the case of foreigners, to return to their native countries, and, in the case of the Chinese soldiers, to go back to their homes. To all this Li agreed, and handsome amounts were paid over to Gordon for distribution in the army. Li, however, felt that, in addition to all this, Gordon's services required some marked recognition at his hands, and through the intervention of Mr. Hart, he invited him to accept a large sum of money. With characteristic disinterestedness Gordon declined the gift, and retired from the command a poorer man than when he took it up. In the meantime Li had presented a memorial to the throne, in which he reported the distinguished services rendered by Gordon in the field, and in response to which the Emperor promoted Gordon to the rank of Ti-Tu (commander-in-chief of a provincial army), and presented him with a yellow jacket, a peacock's feather to be worn on his cap, and four suits of uniform proper to his new rank. These Imperial insignia Gordon accepted.

But though to Li the dissolution of Gordon's force was a subject for congratulation, there was one man who took a very opposite view. Sir Harry Parkes had succeeded to the Consulate at Shanghai, and viewed with concern the disbandment of a force which had been primarily constituted for the protection of that settlement. He felt that such a step should not have been taken by Li without having first consulted him on the subject. This view he urged repeatedly on the Governor in letters, in which he further pointed out that Her Majesty's Government were about to withdraw the British troops which had hitherto garrisoned Shanghai, and that therefore the time chosen for breaking up Gordon's force was singularly inopportune. As it was necessary to come to some understanding in the matter, Li invited Sir Harry to visit him at Soochow, and on this occasion his visitor strongly advocated the establishment of a camp of instruction to be formed in the neighbourhood of Shanghai, and to be placed under the command of British officers.

After some beating about the bush the camp was formed, and Gordon was asked to take the command for the time being. But the whole project was distasteful to Li, who had an uncomfortable way of making his displeasure apparent. He thwarted Gordon, to whom he was so much indebted, at every turn, and in fact made it so unpleasant for him that he determined to resign the post. In a letter to Parkes, Gordon at this time wrote:

"The Futai (Li) has done what I imagine we require, but it has been done in an unpleasant way. . . . . I am convinced of one thing, viz., that it is far better to leave the matter in your hands, than for me to try to accommodate our views with those of the Futai." This was probably true. Sir Harry Parkes was accustomed to carry his points with Chinese mandarins, and even Li, powerful as he was, and with all the prestige of having suppressed the rebellion in Kiangsu, had to yield before him. But he did it with a bad grace, and on the occasion of a second visit paid him at Soochow by Sir Harry Parkes, he showed how much his concessions had cost him by treating his visitor with but scant courtesy. No people know better how to use speech as a weapon with which to wound and insult than Chinamen, and on this occasion Li ruffled the feelings of his visitor by referring to Sir Harry's Order of the Bath by the same name as that which he used to signify "the nondescript ornaments which he himself invented and issued to the foreigners in his employ."

The question of the disciplined force was still the subject of their discussion, and with characteristic subterfuge, Li, while agreeing to Sir Harry's propositions, requested him to arrange the matter with the Chinese general in command. That officer, evidently at a hint from head quarters, took the opportunity of absenting himself, so that when Parkes reached his Yamên he found it untenanted, and learned that he whom he sought had betaken himself to a town twelve miles away. But Parkes was not a man to be put off in this way, and he at once followed in pursuit. On running the general to earth, he was met with the assertion that he was too ill to receive visitors. Recognising that this was only another move in the game, Parkes took up his position in the reception-hall, and told the general's servants that he should wait there till their master was in a fit state to receive him. The result was as Parkes had expected, a complete surrender on the part of the general, who presently appeared in perfect health, though very cross, and finally agreed unconditionally to all Parkes's proposals. The camp of instruction however was not destined to have a long life. The old doggrel—

> "When the devil was sick, the devil a saint would be;
> When the devil was well, the devil a saint was he"—

applies aptly to the government and rulers of China. So long as the rebels were actively in the field, Li was most anxious to enlist the services of foreigners. But so soon as he had swept the T'aip'ings out of his province, he began to regard the presence of foreigners among his troops as a doubtful good. After his usual manner he made his opinions apparent in disagreeable ways, and ultimately the camp was abolished. His experiences had fully demonstrated to Li the superiority of foreign weapons of war, and he considered that they had also

shown the inadvisability of constituting a force which
could in any way be considered to have an independent existence from him.   He therefore determined
to restrict the employment of foreigners to the management of a shell and ammunition factory at Soochow, over
which he appointed Macartney superintendent.   The experiment was successful, and Li had the gratification of
seeing most excellent work done by his own employés.

The miserable condition in which the province had
been left after the suppression of the rebellion, gave Li
abundant opportunity for the exercise of those administrative powers which he possesses in so marked a degree.
He at once set about encouraging the natives to return to
the towns and villages, and he appealed to the Throne to
grant a remission of three years' tribute to the harassed
and impoverished people.   To the restoration of Soochow,
which has always been one of the most beautiful cities in
the empire, he paid especial attention.   He rebuilt the
Yaméns, cleared out the water-courses, which under
the paralyzing rule of the T'aip'ings had been filled
with every kind of abominations, and he established
a postal system between that city and Shanghai for the
convenience of native traders.   He bestowed equal
attention on the sister city of Hangchow, where, if report
speaks truly, he recovered a large quantity of treasure
which had been concealed, probably by some owner or
owners on the approach of the rebels to the town.   There
is in Li as in most Chinamen, a strong sentiment of
superstition, and the discovery of this treasure is said to
have been due to directions imparted to him in a twice-
dreamt dream.   In the same spirit of credulity he

memorialized the throne after the capture of Changchow, asking that special honour should be conferred on Kwanti, the god of war, who had, in answer to his prayers, changed, on the day of the attack, pouring rain into brilliant sunshine, a north to a south wind, and had given increased force and power to the guns and muskets of the Imperial force. His prayer was granted by the Emperor, and a tablet in the temple of the god acknowledges the services which were rendered by his power on the eventful day. With the recovery of Nanking on the 19th July, 1864, the rebellion came to an end, and though Li's efforts for the recovery of that capital had only been indirect, the main glory resting with Tséng Kwofan, the emperor was pleased to create him a *Pih* or earl, in recognition of his services on that memorable occasion. Tséng Kwofan received the honour of a marquisate, which in due course descended to his son, who was sometime minister at the Court of St. James's.

The possession of Nanking determined Li Hungchang to remove thither the arsenal which had been established by Dr. Macartney at Soochow. Being situated on the Yangtsze-Kiang, the recovered city was obviously the best suited to serve as a naval and military centre, and with the removal of the arsenal, fortuitous events brought a welcome addition to the machinery at the disposal of Li. While the T'aip'ing rebellion was at its height the Chinese Government had commissioned Mr. Lay, who was then Inspector General of Customs, to purchase a fleet of gunvessels for service against the rebels. Had not the Li and Gordon forces been so successful as they were, the probability is that these vessels would have taken a useful

part in the campaign. But on the arrival of the ships,
under the command of Captain Sherard Osborn, in 1863,·
the fortunes of the Taip'ings were on the wane, and the
necessity which had prompted the order for the vessels
no longer existed. From the first Captain Osborn encountered the usual difficulties which are the common lot of
foreigners in Chinese service. His ships had no sooner
anchored at Shanghai than Li's emissaries attempted to
induce his men to transfer their services to the provincial
fleets. By the offer of higher rates of pay nearly all the
stokers from one ship were tempted into joining Li's
gunboats, and Captain Osborn was glad to steam northwards, in order to carry his men beyond the reach of
temptation.

Instead, however, of being received at Peking in the
spirit in which Mr. Lay had originally been approached,
Captain Osborn was told that he would be expected to
act under the orders of Li, who would appoint a Chinese
mandarin to advise with him on all matters connected
with the fleet. This was so directly in opposition to the
terms of the agreement under which he had consented to
serve the Chinese Government, that he at once placed on
on record a formal protest against the proposition. The
manner also in which Li had recently behaved to Gordon
further accentuated Captain Osborn's determination to
have nothing to do with the arrangement proposed ; and
in a series of outspoken letters to the Tsungli Yamèn
he made it plain that Li's behaviour in relation to the
Ever-Victorious Army had made it impossible for any
British officer of standing to serve under him.

As the Chinese were incapable of making use of the

ships without foreign help, it was determined to send the fleet to England for sale. There had been sent with them, however, a considerable supply of machinery for the establishment of naval dockyards. This Li was unwilling should pass out of his hands, and it was finally arranged that it should be erected at Nanking, in addition to the works already established by Dr. Macartney. The whole negociations with regard to the fleet and machinery represent the attitude which Li Hungchang has consistently adopted towards foreigners and their skill. He will make use of their mechanical knowledge, and in times of danger and difficulty will put weapons into their hands to fight against the enemies of his country, but he will never trust them with power. It is said that the proposal made by Burgevine to Gordon, that they should together march an army on Peking and possess themselves of the Empire, which was well known to Li, inspired in his mind a deep distrust of all "outer barbarians." But however that may be, it is certain that he has always shown himself distrustful of Europeans, and willing to throw over those whom he has employed as soon as he considers that they have served his purpose. The last instance of this was furnished by the intrigue which obliged Admiral Lang to resign, a few years ago, the command of the Northern Squadron. In this case Li has paid dearly for the indulgence of his suspicions. If Admiral Lang had continued in the command, the battle of Yalu might have had another issue, and the Chinese fleet might have been dominant in the Gulf of Petchili, instead of having been captured and sunk by the Japanese navy.

CHAPTER V.

TO the stirring times of the T'aip'ing Rebellion had now succeeded in Kiangsu piping times of peace, and Li had leisure to devote himself to the peaceful administration of his province. The fierce storms which had swept over the unhappy territory had left the people and their affairs in a disturbed and disastrous condition. It is, however, a fortunate fact, when we consider how often the provinces of China are thrown into disorder by rebellion, floods, and famines, that in no other country does trade recover itself more readily than in the Celestial Empire, and under Li's fostering care prosperity began once again to shed its light on that fertile district. It is not to be supposed that the people settled down peacefully at once. Industries were disturbed by past perturbations and new conditions, and among the boatmen of the province—a large and unruly community—serious discontent broke out at the increased number of foreign steamers which had learned to ply up the Yangtsze during the troublous times of the T'aip'ing Rebellion. These vessels, they complained, were taking the bread out of their mouths, and they asked for redress. Li espoused

their cause, and memorialised the Throne on the subject.
But he was well aware that no open opposition to foreign
steamers, trading under their treaty rights, was possible,
and he could only urge that the conveyance of Government rice should be more strictly confined to the native
crafts than it then was. A man of less powerful will and
determination would have found this and countless other
elements of discontent and disorder which still smouldered
in the province, matters of serious danger. But wherever
Li has been he has invariably made his determination
known to rule with a rod of iron, and the people, who are
by tradition accustomed to a very parental government,
have invariably submitted to him without a murmur.

Li, however, was not destined to continue long at
Nanking. The suppression of the T'aip'ings had not
entirely destroyed the spirit of revolt which had so long
disturbed the central provinces of the empire. The rebels
who for so many years had been accustomed to live on
their fellow-countrymen, and had lost all desire and power
to earn honest livelihoods, were in a great majority of
cases both unable and unwilling to return to the
ordinary duties of citizenship. It is always easy to
live by plunder in China, where the people show a
strange incapacity for protecting themselves against
armed forces, and so it happened that the surviving
remnants of the T'aip'ings who had been driven from
the shores of the Yangtsze reappeared as banditti, under
the name of *Nienfei*, in the provinces of Shantung and
Honan. At first it was believed that the local forces
would have been able to cope with the outbreak. But
this proved not to be the case, and Li was appointed

Imperial Commissioner to suppress the rebellion. His
experience in the T'aip'ing campaign clearly pointed him
out for the post, and now, as then, he turned to foreigners
for help. Having enlisted a sufficient number of those
who had served under him in the earlier rebellion, he
marched northwards in execution of his mission. Like the
southern portion of the province of Kiangsu, Shantung
is bounded, though more decidedly, on three sides—
north, east, and south—by the sea, and Li determined
to carry out the same tactics there that had proved
successful in the southern province. By hemming the
T'aip'ings in against the sea-board, the Imperialists had
succeeded in netting their opponents, and Li now designed
to drive the Nienfei in the same way into the Shantung
promontory, and there to destroy them.

With curious deliberation he erected a barrier across
the promontory, and then advanced against the enemy.
But he had left one element out of his calculations. He
had forgotten that by the aid of junks it would be possible
for the rebels to escape from the trap in which he thought
to secure them, and to his infinite disappointment he
suddenly found that they had turned his line of attack
by the assistance of native vessels, and had marched off
in his rear to "fresh woods and pastures new." Meanwhile
a further promotion devolved upon him. Tsêng Kwofan,
who had occupied the Viceroyalty of Hukwang for some
years, had been promoted to the Viceroyalty of the
two Kiangs, and Li was appointed in his place (1867),
with orders, however, to prosecute the campaign with
renewed energy against the Nienfei. But circumstances
were against the new Viceroy. Unlike the T'aip'ings, the

Nienfei were for the most part mounted, and thus were able to avoid at pleasure the pitched battles in which Li desired to engage them. The light rebel cavalry were always able to keep a day or two in advance of Li's heavy battalions, and they had no sooner escaped from the Shantung promontory than they rode off into Honan, pillaging the towns and villages through which they passed, and always in advance of the Imperialists, who levied a second and still heavier toll on the wretched inhabitants. As was said at the time, "the rebels came like a hailstorm, but the Imperialist soldiers settled down on a district like locusts, destroying every green thing."

Li's want of complete success was severely criticised by the Board of Censors, but the Viceroy was too powerful and too useful a man to be seriously interfered with, and he therefore escaped with a reprimand from the Throne, while his subordinates, the Governor of Hupei and the Treasurer of the province of Shantung, were deprived of their buttons. This rebuke, however, failed in its intended effect, and desultory fighting, ending in no definite results, occupied the next few months. In spite of the reports of victories which from time to time Li presented as a flattering unction to the Throne, the indecisive nature of the campaign exhausted the Imperial patience, and in the following year (1868) he was degraded for apathy, and was ordered to take up his post of Viceroy at Wooch'ang. The futility of an infantry force attempting to crush a body of light cavalry had convinced the Court that the appointment of a Mongol cavalry chieftain, with his following of hardy horsemen, would be more likely to account satisfactorily for the Nienfei than Li's infantry could ever be expected to do. Li, however, was determined not to be set aside, and was able to bring such arguments to bear as to induce the Court to forego the proposed scheme, though he was compelled so far to yield to his enemies as to purchase his continuance in his command by submitting to be degraded three steps in rank. Fortunately for him the wheel of fortune turned, and he was shortly able to report a genuine and decisive victory, which restored him to his former rank, and gave him back the yellow jacket, of which he had been temporarily deprived, and which had been originally conferred upon him with other honours for the part he had played in the T'aip'ing campaign. Having by this and other victories crushed the rebellion in Shantung and Honan, he was summoned to Peking to an Imperial audience, and then proceeded to Wooch'ang to take up the duties of his Viceroyalty.

Li has throughout his career been fond of state and prone to comfort, and the manner in which he journeyed to his post was characteristic of the man. Discarding the wearisome land route, he went by steamer to Shanghai, and here, in deference to the popular feeling among the boatmen which he had fostered when Governor of Kiangsu, he transhipped himself into a native junk. Being, however, unwilling to submit to the normal length of the voyage, he caused his junk to be towed up the Yangtsze by the steamer *T'ungchi*, and thus with the further escort of the steamers *Confucius*, *Pluto*, and *Sycee* he travelled to Wooch'ang.

It was at this time that he wrote the following letter to his old companion in arms, Colonel Gordon, which shows that though there had been many causes of bitterness between them, he could look back with pleasure to their former alliance. The letter, which is quoted from a note to the proceedings of the Royal Artillery Institution, reads as follows :

"To LIEUT.-COLONEL GORDON,

"Late Commander-in-Chief of the Ever-Victorious Army.

"When Colonel Doyle was going home, I enjoined him to enquire as to your welfare, and from your letter lately received, I am fully impressed with the sincerity of your esteem for me, and have to thank you for the interest (undiminished by time and distance) which you continue to take in my doings. I understand that you are at present engaged in erecting batteries, and I have no doubt but that by skill now displayed, you will add to your reputation. I can fully understand the pleasure which the marriage of your sister with Dr. Moffitt must have caused you ; the pleasure must be heightened moreover by the fact of their having settled in the neighbourhood in which you are stationed.

"As regards myself, during last year and the year before (1867 and 1868, T'ung Chi) whilst acting as Imperial Commissioner, I was despatched against the insurgents in the Shantung, Honan, and Chihli Provinces, and as the auspicious halo which surrounds my Imperial Master attended me, my campaign was a successful one. The insurgent chiefs fell into my hands and were destroyed, whilst I had the satisfaction of restoring to liberty several tens of thousands of people who had been compelled to espouse the insurgent cause.

"In the autumn of last year, peace being once more restored, I repaired to the capital, and had an audience with his Imperial Majesty, at the same time being created a joint Assistant Chancellor, still retaining my military command. In the first moon of the present year I entered on my duties as Governor General of 'Hu Kwang.' Lew Mingch'uan has made himself a name, and has been created a baronet. Kwo Sunglin has had a hereditary title conferred on him. Yang Tinghsün, I regret to say, died during the sixth moon of last year; as a mark of Imperial favour a temple is to be erected to his memory. Foreign relations are now on a more satisfactory footing, each country concerning itself about its own affairs. That peace may long continue I fervently join with you in wishing, but if an appeal to arms should at any time become necessary, I shall, while taking the precautions enjoined by you in your note, still be inclined to look to you for aid. The flags of the Ever-Victorious Army are still in my possession. From time to time I have them unfurled for inspection, and whilst they serve to remind me of old times and doings, they also cause my thoughts to wander to you who are so far away. You enquire about the yellow jacket; the decoration was first instituted during the present dynasty for award to Princes, Statesmen, famous Generals, the original recipients being those who fought 'The Three Insurgents,' and reduced once more to allegiance the districts of 'Tsinghai,' 'Ya Kinchawam' (*sic*), 'Teasn Kin Chwan' (*sic*), 'Chun foo,' 'Hwangpoo,' and 'Sin Kiang.' Since the days of 'Heen fung,' those to whom the jacket has been awarded are few in number, whilst of those from western lands, who have assisted China in military matters, you alone, by your loyal and valuable service have been the recipient of this mark of gracious favour. The fact will doubtless be handed down to future generations, and I pride myself with the thought that you will continue to rise to high positions of honour and distinction. I have requested Mr. Hobson to translate and forward this reply, and, wishing you the compliments of the season, I enclose my card, and am,

&c., &c., &c.,

"LI HUNG CHANG."

Li's occupancy of the Viceroyalty of Hu Kwang was not destined to be a long one. But his conduct when there, more especially in his demeanour towards foreigners, was in strict keeping with his previous record. He was willing to make use of them, but he declined altogether to give them any right or privilege which was not enforced by treaty. He would give them their bond, but declined to go one iota beyond the four corners of the document. It so happened that at this time Admiral Keppel was proposing to make a voyage of investigation on the upper waters of the Yangtsze-Kiang. The Admiral was, as Li well knew, a man eminent in his profession and of tried courage and experience. He was one therefore to whom Li, had he been graciously inclined towards foreigners, would have given ready help in any difficulty. But this was not Li's habit, and when Admiral Keppel asked him for the loan of a small steamer to supply the place of the despatch boat in which he had intended going, but which had not arrived, Li declined to grant his request.

In the same spirit he at first attempted to close the front gates of his Yamên to the British Consul, whom he desired should gain admittance by the side doors, appropriated to the lower ranks of Mandarins. When expostulated with on the subject he defended himself by saying that by treaty a Consul was considered to rank with a Taot'ai, and that as Taot'ais were admitted only by the side door, a Consul should not expect the centre gateway to be thrown open to him. Fortunately the Consul declined to visit him on these terms, and eventually Li was obliged to yield, and to receive his visitor in the way which courtesy should have from the first provided for him. The visits of the foreign Consuls were admittedly distasteful to Li, when there was no information which he desired to gain from them ; and in

G

conversation with the British representative at the port, he more than once complained that the frequency of his visits brought him into bad odour with the people. The same admission was made by Prince Kung at a little later period, when he informed Sir Thomas Wade that he and the other ministers of the Tsungli Yamén were "constantly abused on account of their relations with foreigners." It cannot be too often insisted upon that now, as then, this is the attitude of both officials and people towards ourselves. No doubt there are exceptions, but if Li, who more nearly approaches a "progressive" than nine-tenths of the Mandarins, could give vent to such a complaint, it is fair to assume that much stronger sentiments are expressed in private by most of the officials of China.

But Li's stand-off manner towards foreigners was far from being a bar to his receipt of Imperial favours, and in 1869 he was made a Tsai Hsiang or Cabinet Minister for his services against the T'aip'ings and Nienfei rebels. This distinguished promotion brought countless congratulatory letters and messages from friends and colleagues, and even his mother was the recipient of numerous poetical and other laudatory communications. One of these productions in verse ran as follows :

> " Noble lady ! eight-bearer borne ;
> Relict of one distinguished ;
> Mother of many sons ;
> Venerable in years, of family famous ;
> Exalted ! Having in one
> Chief of soldiers and Minister of State ;
> Wondrous attainment of a son !
> Wondrous of a younger son." *

* *The Shanghai Courier.*

Amid his various employments and interests as Viceroy of Hu Kwang Li was not unmindful of the arsenal at Nanking, over which Dr. Macartney presided. He constantly corresponded with that officer, who in response to an invitation, paid the Viceroy a visit at Wooch'ang. So gratified was Li with the report which Dr. Macartney brought him of the work being done, that he ordered a considerable enlargement of the arsenal to be undertaken. As Nanking was beyond the limits of his jurisdiction, it might have been expected that his authority over it would have ceased, but it had been his own creation and was still regarded as his special care. In the same way the lead which he had taken in military affairs had marked him out as the chief power available against all disorders and rebellions. The suppression of the Nienfei had by no means pacified the empire. In the South-Western Provinces of Kweichow and Yunnan a rebellious spirit had long been abroad, and serious outbreaks, which ended in the establishment of a Mahommedan kingdom in Yunnan, were disturbing the peace of the district. So serious was the disaffection that Li Hungchang received orders to proceed at once to suppress the rising spirit of revolt.

It was well known that this task was peculiarly distasteful to the Viceroy. The districts were comparatively little known, the people and border tribes were of a peculiarly turbulent disposition, and the localities had an evil repute for unhealthiness. Li, however, could only murmur and prepare to obey, and he was on the point of setting out on his unpleasant mission, when a further order reached him from Peking directing him to proceed, post haste, to

the Province of Shensi, where certain rebels had gained a
series of victories over the troops led by Tso Tsung-tang.
This officer was well known as an able General, according
to Chinese lights. It was he who subsequently conducted
a remarkable campaign against Kashgaria and recovered
that province for his Imperial master. It will be
remembered that on that occasion he marched across
Central Asia and supplied his troops with the grain
that was sown and reaped on the march. Such leisurely
tactics might be successful against the distant dependency
of Kashgaria, but a General of so dilatory a habit was
plainly not the man to cope with a nimble enemy, who
was within easy striking distance of the capital. Li was
therefore appointed *vice* Tso, and in a very short time
reduced the province to order.

CHAPTER VI.

MEANWHILE, a terrible tragedy occurred at the treaty port of Tientsin. For some months, in the beginning of 1870, there had been an effervescence of popular feeling on the subject of missionaries in various parts of the empire. At Nanking and in other centres disturbances had occurred, and reports were rife at Tientsin of an intended uprising against foreigners. The old popular rumours were scattered broadcast. The missionaries were accused of kidnapping children, for the purpose of using their eyes and other parts of their bodies as drugs. The currency of these rumours was repeatedly brought to the notice of Chung How, the principal mandarin on the spot, who, however, could not be induced to take any steps to suppress them. For some days prior to the 21st June, excited mobs had surrounded the orphanage presided over by sisters of charity, crying out that the sisters were buying children to scoop out their eyes. In the absence of all official opposition the fury of the mob became uncontrollable. On the morning of the 21st the fire brigades beat their gongs to summon the people, who,

as though previously informed, marched directly on the
French Cathedral and Consulate.   In an amazingly short
time these buildings were wrecked, the French Consul
and priests were murdered, and the mob, with their
appetite whetted by the taste of blood, marched on to
the orphanage, where, with relentless cruelty, they murdered the sisters, who had been devoting their lives to the
welfare of the people.   The crisis was one which plainly
demanded the presence of a man of power.   Tsêng
Kwofan was the Viceroy of the Metropolitan Province,
but he was an old man, and pronounced anti-foreign
proclivities marked him as one unfitted to deal with
the present circumstances.   By a curious coincidence,
as though the spirit of murder was abroad, the Viceroy
of the two Kiang Provinces was, at this juncture,
assassinated by a soldier while returning from a military
parade.   The transfer from the Viceroyalty of the
Metropolitan Province to that of any other province
or provinces is unquestionably a descent, but the present
crisis was such that strong measures were necessary,
and Tsêng Kwofan was despatched to Nanking to make
way for Li Hungchang in the province of Chihli.

The new appointment was a marked success.   Li
arrived at Tientsin, preceded and accompanied by a
large force of southern troops.   The people were still
in a disturbed condition of excitement, and Li saw that
it was necessary to make his presence felt at once.   He,
therefore, issued a proclamation, in which he warned the
people that any disturbances would be met by prompt
and vigorous measures.   He reminded them that he had
known how to deal with the best troops led by the

T'aip'ing commanders; that he had successfully quelled the Nienfei Rebellion; that his right hand had not lost its force; and that his troops were loyally prepared to act now, as ever, at his bidding.

The Imperial decree appointing Li to his new post ran thus—

"We command Li Hungchang, who has been translated to the Government-General of Chihli, to proceed post to Tientsin, there, in concert with Tsêng Kwofan, Ting Jihch'ang, and Cheng Lin, to conduct the inquiry still open, and take the necessary action. . . . Respect this."

Though it is plain from this decree that it was intended by the Court that Li should act in concert with Tsêng Kwofan and his colleagues, it soon became obvious that the sole control of affairs rested in his hands. From the first he took a decided line in support of the policy pursued by the Chinese Government. A strong feeling had been expressed, both by official and non-official foreigners, that the prefect and magistrate of Tientsin should be condemned to death for the parts they had played in instigating the outbreak. It was well known, however, that though the Government might not be unwilling to sacrifice victims among the people, a steadfast stand would be made against executing anyone wearing an official button.

In an interview which Mr. Consul Adkins held with Li on the subject of the outbreak, the Viceroy, in response to the consul's expressed opinion that the government had shown very little disposition to act vigorously in the matter, repudiated the imputation somewhat warmly.

"The prefect and magistrate," he said, "had been dismissed; eighty people had been arrested, of whom from twenty-five to thirty would suffer the extreme penalty of the law; others had escaped for the time, but would eventually be brought to justice; the damage done to missionary establishments would be made good, and a special commissioner was about to leave for France to express in the name of the Emperor of China the most sincere regret at the unfortunate occurrences of the 21st of June."

When pressed as to whether he considered dismissal a sufficient punishment for men who were practically responsible for the lives of some twenty foreigners, Li admitted after some fencing that they were worthy of punishment, but this only because a foreign consul had been among the killed. Had the sufferers only been missionaries or traders, dismissal would, in his opinion, have been quite sufficient to meet the requirements of the case.

But the prefect and magistrate were not the only officials whom Li was anxious to protect. A very stormy petrel, who was a protegé of both Tsêng Kwofan and Li, had taken a somewhat prominent part in the outbreak of the 21st of June. Ch'ên Kwojui, who had begun his career as a T'aip'ing rebel, had been induced to join the Imperial standard by the promise of rank. On many occasions he served his new masters with distinction, and was a prime favourite with both Tsêng and Li. His aversion to foreigners was pronounced, and it so happened that his presence had synchronized with anti-foreign outbreaks at Nanking, Yangchow, and other places. Chance brought him to Tientsin in June, 1870, and on the day of the riot it is unquestioned that he urged on the mob in their work of destruction. By his own account he only joined the rioters on being told falsely that Monsieur Fontanier, the French consul, had shot Chung How, the Chinese superintendent of foreign trade. In Li's opinion this account quite exonerated Ch'ên from all blame in the matter. Prince Kung, in a letter addressed to Monsieur de Rochechouart, the French Minister at Peking, took, however, another line in defence of the erring general. "It was by accident," wrote the Prince, 'that the General Ch'ên Kwojui was present at Tientsin. That officer was sick and on a voyage ; he had nothing to do with what took place. There is, therefore, no necessity for saying more on this subject."

This view was contradicted by the evidence of Ch'ên himself, and the case against him was partially confirmed by the admission made to Mr. Wade by a member of the Tsungli Yamên to the effect that "some idle words" had been undoubtedly used by the gallant general on the occasion in question. But from Li's point of view Ch'ên was taboo, and he refused to discuss any imputations against him. So complete was the accused's immunity from all official stigma, that after the massacre he was received in audience by the Emperor, and is said to have returned to Tientsin in the entourage of Li. As to the Tsungli Yamên, the attitude of that body had been throughout the whole discussion most unsatisfactory. It was at this time that the system of trifling with the foreign ministers, which has since been brought to such a state of perfection, was first put into practice. It was difficult to induce the members of the Yamên to discuss any topic more serious than the gossip of the capital, and

by a skilful arrangement of references from one to the
other, and of writing reiterative despatches which were
only intended to promote delay, they succeeded in bringing diplomatic business to a deadlock.   In despair of
furthering negotiations in Peking, Monsieur de Rochechouart, the French Minister, had recourse to Li, and
found, as has been universally acknowledged since, that
however difficult the Viceroy might be to deal with, it
was far easier to arrange matters with him than with the
Yamên.   The French Minister therefore transferred the
scene of his negotiations to Tientsin.   After lengthy but
not unfriendly discussions the following proposals were
made by Li and were accepted by Monsieur de Rochechouart : The payment of an indemnity of 250,000 taels,
120,000 of which was to be paid to the relatives of the
French consul and four other French subjects murdered,
and 130,000 taels for the purposes of the church ; the
banishment of the prefect and magistrate : the execution
of twenty ringleaders of the mob ; and the banishment
of twenty-five others to the Amoor.   This arrangement
was carried out, the money was paid, and the malefactors
were duly beheaded and transported.   By the direction
of Li the execution took place at 5.30 a.m., and as the
month was October, this was of course before dawn.
His professed object for choosing this unusual hour was
to avoid any demonstration among the people ; but the
circumstances which attended the execution would make
it rather appear that it was designed to conceal, as far
as possible, all knowledge of the infliction of the
punishment.

An official messenger who was sent by the consul

to observe what took place, reported that about two hundred police and soldiers had escorted the prisoners from the jail to the court-house.

"None of them would kneel," he added, "to be bound when ordered to do so. They were all dressed in what is everywhere stated to be a Government present, viz., new silk clothes, and wore on their feet shoes of elegant manufacture. Their hair was dressed after the female fashion in various modes, and ornaments such as those seen on the heads of Chinese ladies were stuck in their head-dresses . . . On the way to the execution ground, the criminals bawled out to the crowd, which even at that early time of the morning had collected, 'Have we changed countenance?' and were immediately answered that they had not. They also accused the Chinese authorities of selling their heads to the foreigners, and called out to the people to honour them with the name of 'Brave Boys,' which was done by the united voices of the crowd. A large number of the personal friends and relatives of the condemned followed them along, giving vent to tears and lamentations. On the arrival of the procession at the execution ground, outside the West gate, the criminals commenced singing, on hearing which the presiding magistrate gave the order for their decapitation. The criminals themselves stretched out their necks to receive the blow, and the executioners, all of whom were Southern soldiers, soon finished the proceedings." *

The conclusion thus arrived at was to the Chinese Government a welcome solution of the difficulty, and probably to no one was it more so than to Li Hungchang. From the first he had recognised the possibility that France might enforce her demands for reparation at the point of the bayonet; and though the outbreak of the Franco-German war had lessened the likelihood of such an eventuality, he had deemed it wise to make armed

* *Parliamentary Paper. China. No. 1 (1871).*

preparations to resist a possible invasion by way of the
Peiho.   He re-armed the Taku forts with Krupp guns,
strengthened the earthworks at the mouth of the river,
and added some well constructed and carefully concealed forts between Taku and Tientsin.   As in all his
military difficulties he had recourse on this occasion also
to Dr. Macartney, who visited him at Tientsin and gave
him counsel as to the necessary improvements in the
arsenal which Li had established at Tientsin.   Of this
arsenal Li had been appointed Director by the Emperor,
and had also succeeded Ch'ung How as Superintendent
of trade for the three northern forts.   But these were not
the only additional distinctions which had been showered
upon him.   By Imperial favour he was nominated an
Honorary Imperial Tutor of the second class, Super-
numerary Member of the Great Council of the Empire,
was decorated with the Peacock's feather with Two Eyes,
and was made a Noble of the first class.

Li was thus one of the most decorated Mandarins in
the empire, and by the accumulation of forces attached
especially to his command, he had established himself so
firmly as a power that sinister reports passed current from
time to time to the effect that he harboured ambitious
designs against the Throne.   But on this point his conduct has been straightforward and consistent throughout.
He has ever been a strenuous supporter of the present
Manchu dynasty, and through good report and evil report
he has accepted absolutely the orders of the Son of
Heaven.

The confidence which in return has been placed in him
has for years constituted him the leading statesman in

the empire. His position at Tientsin—which is, as it were, the portal of the capital—has thrust upon him the management to a great extent of foreign affairs. Since his appointment to the Viceroyalty of Chihli no foreign minister or high foreign official has passed through Tientsin without calling upon the great Viceroy. His willingness to receive foreign guests has been proverbial, and his skill in extracting information from his visitors has amply repaid him for the time expended in his receptions. Ministers and distinguished officers who have gone to his Yamén expecting to learn something from him have come away without any addition to their previous stock of knowledge, and with the consciousness superadded that they have been "pumped" most exhaustively by their astute host. It has often been a matter of surprise that Li could find leisure to concern himself with foreign politics, and at the same time conduct the multifarious affairs of the Metropolitan Province. His memorials to the throne, as published in the *Peking Gazette,* furnish curious illustrations of the varied phases of his mind, and the complex nature of his duties. In the year of which we are speaking (1871) disastrous floods inundated large tracts of the province, and Li appealed to the throne for help. This was insufficient, and he asked for permission to apply to the provinces of Kiangsu and Che Kiang, where his prowess against the T'aip'ings was still remembered with gratitude. Happily, the rain ceased before the Grand Canal—which like the Yellow River has in process of time so silted up that the bed is above the level of the surrounding country—overflowed its banks. The return of fine weather was heralded, according to Li, by the appearance in the canal of a river snake, which was at once deified as the Dragon King, and was reverently placed in a temple, where the Viceroy and his subordinates did homage to the beneficent God. But though willing to bow himself before a deified snake, Li was conscious of the futility of trusting for safety for the future to any such miraculous interpositions. The flood had warned him of a great danger, and he, therefore, again memorialised the throne, pointing out the importance of the work to be done, and the insufficiency of the fund provided for the purpose. A considerable sum was annually entered for the repair of the canal in the Imperial Budget, but after the common Chinese practice the sum actually paid amounted only to 25 per cent. of the money allocated for the work, and Li urged that it would be impossible, with less than 40 per cent. of the original sum, to keep the banks in order. This concession was granted him, and he set to work to strengthen the embankments. Before long he was able to report to the throne the completion of the work, which, he averred, had been done for some "myriads of taels" less than on previous occasions, and in virtue of this fact he asked for the promotion of the officials who had contributed to so satisfactory a result. Unhappily, however, for Li, a recurrence of heavy rain brought down so great a flood of water in the canal that it overthrew his embankments, and inundated the country far and wide. This was an opportunity for any hostile censor who might desire to have a fling at the great Viceroy. There were no lack of men so disposed, for Li's power and prominent position had gained for him, as is always the case, more especially in oriental countries, a host of virulent enemies.

So soon as the disaster became known, a censor named Pien took up his ready pen, and appealed with vehemence to the throne, to ask whether Li had not been trifling with his Imperial Master when he reported the safety of the banks, which, at the very first flood, had been swept away, and he confidently demanded the punishment and degradation of Li and his subordinates. The case was too strong and palpable to be resisted, and the subordinate provincial mandarins were awarded the fate proposed by Pien, while Li himself was handed over to the Board of Civil Office for nominal punishment. To this decree Li was obliged to submit, but the annoyance of the attack made him more than ever determined to recover his reputation, and to foil the malice of the censor. With characteristic energy he employed the best engineering skill within reach, and at a considerable cost finally did what he had previously reported had been done. In triumph he announced his success to the throne, and, in accordance with the usual custom, he and all his subordinates who had been degraded were restored to their former ranks, and even had added unto them "Flowered Peacock Feathers."

But Censor Pien had another string to his bow. Li in a moment of superstitious reverence had addressed a memorial to the Emperor, announcing the appearance of some stalks of double-eared wheat within his province, and foretelling that as in the time of Yao, (2356 B.C.) so now, this manifestation was the sign of the conspicuous goodwill of Heaven towards the

Emperor. All this Pien denounced as adulatory
nonsense. Such stalks of wheat, were, he asserted,
constantly to be met with, and he further added that
instead of carrying any heavenly significance they
proved only that the soil on which they grew was
unusually fertile. He deplored that a man of Li's
eminence should stoop to such folly, and begged that
in order to stop the practice of reporting such coinci-
dences, Li's memorial should be characterised in the
manner which it deserved. He even hinted that Li's
real object was not so much to emphasize the approval
of Heaven of the Emperor's rule, as to bring into prominence the excellence of his own Government. In
this case, however, Pien was not so successful as in
his previous attack, and no censure was pronounced in
accordance with his prayer.

On countless other subjects Li presented endless
memorials, as the *Peking Gazettes* of that same year bear
testimony. Was any old officer who had served under
him against the T'aip'ings in distress he was sure of gaining Li's support, and in case of his death his relatives
were gratified by Li's strenuous efforts to gain posthumous
honours for the deceased. If any old lady or gentleman
should be fortunate enough to have seen seven generations, she or he could look confidently for procuring the
erection of the honorific gateway which is so much prized
as the Imperial recognition of private virtue. Should any
son or daughter show an extraordinary degree of filial
piety Li was always ready to gain the Imperial approval of
the virtuous young person. As an instance of his action
in such matters a single case may be mentioned. A

young lady within his jurisdiction had, he assured the Son of Heaven, shown from her earliest years a complete devotion to her parents. On the occasion of an illness which overtook her mother this young lady cut a piece of flesh from her arm to make soup for the recovery of her parent. The remedy answered to her highest hopes, and on the unfortunate recurrence of the malady she was encouraged to repeat the experiment,—this time by the mutilation of her leg, in the expectation of the same happy result. But fate was adverse, and the old lady died. Her daughter's grief was piteous to behold, and recognising that life was no longer endurable, she dressed herself with unusual care, and having ascended a neighbouring pagoda, threw herself from the height. Such an instance of filial piety should not, in Li's opinion, be passed over in silence, and he asked that a tablet inscribed by the Imperial hand should be presented to the surviving relatives. This was done, and the memory of the fair devotee stands recorded for ever in the ancestral hall of the family.*

At times Li's memorials of this same period were anything but pleasant reading for those to whom they referred. Incompetent magistrates were denounced in short and incisive terms, and on the Chinese principle of interdependent responsibility magistrates were constantly degraded and dismissed, on his recommendation, for having in their employ jailors and others who had failed in their duties. Another memorial represents a thoroughly characteristic trait of Chinese officialdom. Li reported to the throne that a degraded general had

* *Peking Gazette*, June 11, 1873.

given a thousand taels towards the relief of the sufferers from the flood, and on this ground procured for the peccant officer the restoration of his honours, including the Peacock feather, which had previously adorned his hat. But even among these varied occupations Li found time for schemes of more than a purely administrative character. He informed his Imperial master that it was his intention to superintend the re-editing of the History of the Imperial Domain. The last edition had been brought out a hundred and forty years before. There was much therefore to record in that interval, and besides, in Li's opinion former editions had been guilty of inserting much unnecessary material. He reminded the Emperor that Buddhism and Taoism were heterodox creeds, Confucianism being the only orthodox faith, and he found fault therefore with the insertion of the biographies of noted Buddhist and Taoist priests in earlier editions of the work. This is thoroughly characteristic of Li. He is a Confucianist to the backbone, and being bound by the chains of an intensely reactionary faith, his sympathies have become narrowed and his mind warped, until it may truly be said that he has become one who

> " Though born for the Universe, narrowed his mind,
>   And to party gave up what was meant for mankind."

Another scheme which he laid at the foot of the Throne was one with no such literary interest, but was designed in a spirit directly hostile to foreign enterprise in China. The condition of the Yellow River and of the southern portion of the Grand Canal had been such as to cause considerable anxiety to the government. The canal on which Peking depended for its supply of southern grain had been so long and so completely neglected that it was fast becoming unnavigable, and numerous memorials had been presented to the Throne by provincial officials, recommending schemes for clearing out the bed. In a long memorial Li reviewed all these recommendations, and advised that one and all should be disregarded in favour of a proposal that the native mercantile marine should be encouraged and developed. This met with approval, and Li at once proceeded to carry out a scheme which he had long meditated, of forming a company of native merchants, who should purchase foreign steamers which, by virtue of the privileges belonging to them as being native-owned, would be able to compete successfully with the foreign lines. In pursuance of this policy the "China Merchants' Steam Navigation Company" came into existence, and Li announced its formation in the following proclamation :

"Whereas, under the cognisance of the Throne, at my instance, a Board has been established to invite merchants to run steamers, as an experiment, for the transport of the grain tribute, and at the same time for freight and passenger traffic between the ports, the head office being at Shanghai, with branches for the furtherance of these objects at Tientsin, Canton, Hongkong, Foochow, Hankow, Kinkiang, Chinkiang, Ningpo, Yentai, and Newchwang. And whereas Chinese merchant craft should properly pay dues at the old-established maritime customs-houses, license has been obtained from the superintendents of those customs-houses to allow steamers and sailing vessels of foreign build, on changing to the Chinese flag, for greater convenience and economy to pass their goods through the new maritime customs, and pay according to the foreign scale. This system has been communicated to the Tsungli Yamên, and has been carried into effect by the said Board. And whereas Chinese merchants, living as they do at various distances from the ports, may not all be acquainted with the facts, this proclamation is issued to let them know that, as to merchandise shipped by the China Merchants' Steam Navigation Company, if the shipper carries on business within the concession the duties must be paid at the new maritime customs ; if without the concession, the duties demanded at every Imperial barrier and Lekin station must as heretofore be paid. Any wilful infringement of this, with the intention of evading duties, will subject the goods to confiscation and the trader to rigorous punishment according to law. Let all obey with trembling."

Thus was launched a scheme which was destined to an uncertain and chequered existence. Chinese merchants have a profound and well-grounded suspicion of any undertaking that is under official guidance, and later on we shall have to record the difficulties of this enterprise, notwithstanding the powerful patronage of Li.

CHAPTER VII.

BUT after all, Li's most important duties were connected with the office he held of Commissioner
for Foreign Affairs. During the time when the matters
connected with the Tientsin massacre were under discussion, Li had been haunted with the idea that war
was always possible, and he had seen enough during
the T'aip'ing rebellion to know that his country was quite
unprepared to face a European foe. He exerted himself
therefore to the utmost to strengthen the defences of the
capital, and to provide himself with as effective an army
and navy as possible. In furtherance of this object he
armed and drilled a large force of Honan soldiers, whom
he kept within his province, and he acquired from time
to time foreign gunboats for the protection of the coasts.
Even at this time (1872) the advances made by Japan
were causing him some anxiety. He watched with
apprehension the adoption of foreign systems in the
Japanese army and navy, and he felt that before long
the time would come when Japan would attempt to
measure her strength against his Chinese battalions.

But the time was not yet, and meanwhile it became his duty to enter into a diplomatic struggle with a less dangerous foe.

Peru, of all countries in the world, desired to make a treaty with China, and Captain Garcia y Garcia was sent on a mission to negotiate the terms. But his task was not a light one. For some years his countrymen had been carrying on a system of Chinese emigration from Macao, which, in the opinion of the Chinese authorities, amounted to nothing more nor less than a practice of kidnapping into slavery. When, therefore, the envoy opened negotiations with Li, he was met by a statement of conditions which he found it extremely difficult either to accept or to denounce as unjust. Li insisted that all Chinese coolies at Peru should be released from their engagements, and that those who wished to return to China should be sent home at the expense of the Peruvian Government; that any future emigrants going to Peru should be as unfettered in their actions as American, British, or German subjects would be under the same conditions; and that no emigrants should be shipped from Macao for the future. With some modifications Captain Garcia y Garcia was obliged to accept these proposals, and after the delay of many months a treaty was finally agreed upon, and signed by Li on the part of China, and by Captain Garcia y Garcia on that of Peru.

Already Japan, in virtue of her newly-established freedom, had claimed the right of making a treaty with China, and on the appearance of the Japanese Minister Taneomi Soyeshima, Li had brought vividly before him the advance which had been made by China's progressive neighbour. The Viceroy's astonishment at the appearance of the Envoy in European clothes was amusingly great, and his angry contempt at the desertion it implied from Oriental associations was proportionately deep. It required some self-restraint to admit without cavil Japan's claim of equality with China. In past history Japan had always been regarded as a tributary state, and even up to the time of the appearance of Taneomi Soyeshima at Li's Yamên a *quasi* air of superiority had been invariably assumed by China towards the Land of the Rising Sun. Now, however, so far as a treaty could make them, they were destined to be pronounced to be on terms of equality. By the Articles of the Treaty they were each bound to aid and support the other in case of an attack by a foreign power, and it was provided also that each should send Ministers to the capital of the other, and appoint Consuls to protect the interests of their nations at the treaty ports of both countries. After some negotiation the terms were mutually agreed to, and on the 30th April, 1873, the ratifications were exchanged at Tientsin, Li again representing his Imperial master.

The relations thus entered into were destined in the following year (1874) to be subjected to an unusually severe strain. The island of Formosa has always presented administrative difficulties to its Chinese rulers. While the western portion of the island is comparatively civilized and is directly under the control of the Chinese Mandarins, the mountainous districts on the eastern shore are inhabited by wild tribes, who have never given in more than a nominal adhesion to the Chinese sovereignty.

The mode of life of these tribes is primitive in the extreme, and one of their principal means of existence is derived from their calling as wreckers. In that typhoon-tossed sea numberless ships are annually driven as hopeless wrecks on the shores of the island. Such salvage goods as supply the wants of the natives are appropriated without question, and the lives of any sailors who may escape to the shore are commonly forfeited. It so happened that in the early part of 1874 a Japanese vessel was cast up on the inhospitable shore of the island, as many had been before, and the crew were murdered as a matter of course.

In ordinary times such a familiar incident would have been allowed to pass without question; but the Japanese, who are essentially a military nation, were just beginning to feel the pride and power begotten by a military system organised on the European method. The Samurai and their followers, who had been accustomed in bygone days to the constant civil wars which had broken the peaceful epochs of the nation's history into very short lengths, had temporarily exchanged the pleasure of cutting one another's throats for the gratification felt in acquiring the knowledge of foreign tactics and arms. With an acquaintance with these accessories of power came a desire to try their efficiency, and the murder of a few Japanese subjects in Formosa furnished an opportunity of bringing their value to the test of experience. A large and powerful party in the state, headed by Okubo, looked with disfavour upon this filibustering spirit. But the aggressive party was too strong for them, and explanations were demanded from China of the outrages

committed by the Formosan savages. With that short-
sighted policy which has so often of late years proved
fatal to Chinese diplomacy, the Tsungli Yamên declared
that the savages of Formosa were practically beyond the
jurisdiction of the Chinese Government. This declaration furnished the war party in Japan with the excuse
which they wanted for taking action, and as the mouth-
piece of this party the Government declared that since
this was so, they would take the matter into their own
hands. In pursuance of this policy they landed a force
on the island of Formosa, and entered upon a campaign
against the aboriginal tribes. This action was sufficiently
pronounced to make it necessary for Japan to send a
Commissioner to Peking to explain the proceeding. This
appointment was conferred on Soyeshima, who in due
course arrived at Tientsin, and, as is the custom, called
upon Li, whom he found prepared to take the initiative
in the negotiations into his own hands. But Li was
yet to learn that the Japanese were astute enough to
frustrate any attempt to interfere with their negotiations
with the Central Government, and strong enough to disregard the anger of even so considerable an authority as
himself. On the occasion of the visit of the Commissioner, Li, as is his wont in such cases, attempted
to draw him into a political discussion, and in course of
his remarks handed him a paper on which was written
a saying of Confucius, condemnatory of "the lawless
encroachment of one state upon the territories of
another." But Soyeshima was equal to the occasion.
He passed lightly by Li's political disquisitions, and
even threw cold water on the dictum of the ancient

sage. His instructions were, he said, not to enter on
any discussion of the subject in dispute until he reached
Peking, and so took his leave, to the intense annoyance
of his host, who is not a man who can easily forgive a
diplomatic defeat.

The deliberations which were carried on at Peking
were thoroughly characteristic of the Chinese Government,
and were almost identical in their procedure with those
which preceded the late war. At first the Chinese took a
high hand, and scouted the idea of making any arrangement until the Japanese had, as a preliminary measure,
withdrawn from Formosa. So soon, however, as they
found that the Japanese were unmoved by this uncom-
promising attitude, the members of the Tsungli Yamên
began to haunt the Foreign Legations, and in a vacillating
way to ask with one breath for the mediation of the
Powers, and with the next that facilities might be given
them for the purchase of ships and guns. Sir Thomas
Wade's description of his part in these negotiations is extremely amusing. The Chinese wavered so continually
between peace and war that the Minister was fairly
puzzled as to their ultimate intentions, and, in order
to clear the way, he put to Prince Kung in writing, the
following questions : "Whether the Chinese really
desired arbitration at all ? If so, what point would
be submitted to the arbitrators ? Whether there was
ground for believing that the Japanese would agree to
arbitration ? Whether the Chinese Government had
made any overtures, and, if so, what, to the Japanese ?
What course, if a rupture ensued, the Chinese Government would follow ?" These questions were far too

direct for the Chinese in their present mood, or rather moods, to answer.

Li, it was well known, was strongly opposed to any compromise with the Japanese. He had provided himself with ships, he had armed his troops with the best rifles of the day, and he believed that at that moment he was in a better position to fight than the Japanese were. He further recognised that the Japanese were moving far faster than his countrymen were ever likely to advance, and that though the Japanese might not then be as powerful as the Chinese, the time would assuredly come when they would be too formidable a foe to make it safe for the Chinese to cross swords with them. At Peking, however, the peace party was in the ascendant, and the negotiations gradually tended towards a peaceful solution of the difficulty. By degrees it became customary to speak of an indemnity to be paid by the Chinese for the expenses entailed by the expedition, and the matter gradually dwindled down to a question of the amount of the payment. The Japanese Commissioner mentioned 3,000,000 taels, as a sum which would induce the Japanese to evacuate Formosa. This amount the Chinese declared to be exorbitant, and they were still haggling over the number of taels which they were to pay for the recovery of their own territory when Okubo appeared at Peking as High Commissioner, with powers to take up the negotiations. The arrival of this diplomat was a guarantee for the peaceful solution of the difficulty, and after some negotiations he agreed to accept 500,000 taels as a recompense to Japan for the expenses of the raid.

So far matters had gone comparatively smoothly, but as the money was not to be paid down on the nail Okubo asked for some guarantee that the stipulated sum would be forthcoming. This the Chinese haughtily declined to give, and Okubo was on the point of breaking off negotiations when Sir Thomas Wade, in the interests of peace, declared himself ready on his personal responsibility to guarantee the payment of the money. Peace was thus restored, much to the gratification of Prince Kung and his colleagues, but to the disappointment of Li, who felt that he had lost an opportunity of putting his warlike preparations to the proof.

Though the Chinese Government had been obliged to yield, so far as paying compensation was concerned, to the invaders, they were extremely averse to making any public admission of the fact, and the articles of the agreement were drawn up in terms which were expecially intended to save their *amour propre.* They were worded with such curious care to this end that they are worth quoting :

"In the matter of the savages of Formosa, reference being had to an understanding arrived at with the two governments [of China and Japan] by the British Minister, Mr. Wade, and to the instrument this day signed, recording the action to be taken respectively by the two parties thereto, the Chinese Government will at once give the sum of 100,000 taels to compensate the families of the shipwrecked Japanese who were killed. In addition to this, the Chinese Government will not fail to pay a further sum of 400,000 taels on account of the expenses occasioned by the construction of roads and erection of buildings which, when the Japanese troops are withdrawn, the Chinese Government will retain for its own use."* etc.

* *Parliamentary Paper. China.* No. 2 (1875).

If the Chinese Government were anxious to conceal the true nature of the compromise in the official documents, they were still more desirous of preventing all knowledge of their having succumbed from reaching the nation at large. The *Peking Gazette* was therefore silent on the subject of the negotiations, and the only mention of Formosa that occurs in the Gazette about this period is a casual statement in a memorial on another subject to the effect that, " Besides this, the Japanese being at present engaged in a warlike enterprise against the aborigines of Formosa, it is necessary to provide in all directions for coast defences." Some months afterwards, with a curious touch of national conceit, an Imperial edict was published, conferring honours and distinctions on native generals who were reported to have conducted successful campaigns against the savages conquered by the Japanese — an instance of vicarious conquest which is not altogether uncommon in Chinese official documents. But though the *Gazette* was silent on the Formosan difficulty, it was full of numerous memorials from Li Hungchang, in reference to the administration of his province. The Emperor and Empresses decreed that they would visit their ancestral tombs in the spring of 1874, and as these are situated within the province of Chihli, it became Li's duty to go as a forerunner to make straight the road, and to smooth the rough places, along the eighty miles which separate Peking from the mausolea. On the 10th April the Imperial procession moved out of the palace, and the *Gazette* tells us that at the first halting-place Li presented his Imperial master with fruits and a *Hwang Hwa* fish — a fish which is said to appear only in the

fourth month of the year, and which the people are
forbidden to eat until one has been presented at the
Imperial table. After the same manner Li attended at
the various halting-places, and offered vegetables with
condiments to stimulate the appetite of the Emperor, and
perchance of the Empresses.

But his duties connected with the progress were by
no means concluded with the return of the Emperor to
the palace. The purveyors of camels, carts, and horses
had repeatedly been late in starting, and had to be
dealt with by the Viceroy. Petitioners also had on
several occasions presented memorials to the Emperor
by the roadside. Some of the complaints contained in
these documents were well-founded, and showed a remarkable laxity in the conduct of local affairs. But the nature
of the complaints had nothing in the world to do with the
punishments inflicted. In each case the penalty of a
hundred blows and penal servitude was meted out to
the offenders. Other memorials by Li bring into prominence the intense cruelties inflicted on culprits in the
name of justice. In three cases during the year 1874
Li reported to the Throne the infliction of the capital
sentence of *Lingchi*, or as it is commonly spoken of,
"Slicing into a thousand pieces," and added that in one
instance he had personally presided at the execution. In
each case the crime was either parricide or matricide, and
in one instance an additional feature of horror attaches to
the sentence, from the fact that the culprit was a lunatic,
who was quite unaccountable for his actions. By the
law of China derangement of mind is no excuse for crime.
Another case in which this barbarous sentence was carried

out affords a curious instance of the intricacies of Chinese law. Li reported that a dissipated youth, who had given his parents infinite trouble, aggravated his offences by stealing from the house a hoe which he pawned, and which his mother redeemed. A second time he carried off the hoe, but this time in the presence of his mother, who followed him with loud outcries, demanding the return of the implement. His father hearing the uproar, came on the scene just in time to receive on his head a blow from a stone which the youth had thrown at his mother. Death ensued, and the sentence of lingchi was passed. Now comes the curious part of the story. So soon as the son's trial had been disposed of, his mother was charged with having so provoked her son as to incite him to cause the death of his father, and for this offence she was sentenced to receive thirty blows with the bamboo!

Towards the end of the year the empire was alarmed by the news that on the day of the transit of Venus (December 9th), the Emperor had been attacked with small-pox. At first the malady was said to have been slight, and it being believed that the danger was over, the Imperial physicians were promoted to high honours. At the opening of the year, however (1875), the disease took a turn for the worse, and on the 12th January the Emperor, in the grandiloquent phrase used on such occasions, "ascended on a dragon to be a guest on high." Then followed one of those intrigues which are common in Eastern courts. It was possible that the young Empress widow might have born a son who would have been heir to the throne, in which case she would

naturally have been proclaimed Regent. This would
have snatched all power from the hands of the two
elder dowager Empresses who had ruled during the long
minority of the late Emperor. Evil was therefore
determined against the young widow, who sickened and
died, her child being yet unborn. The report published
that she had died of grief was received with the
incredulity which it deserved, and colour was given to
the popular version of the story, by the fact that
immediately on the decease of the Emperor the
dowager Empresses nominated the infant son of Prince
Ch'un, a brother of the penultimate Emperor, Hienfung,
to the throne, a sovereign who still continues to reign.
Some reparation was plainly due to the poor lady who
had been thus put out of the way, and Li Hungchang
addressed the following memorial to the throne, recommending that many and adulatory titles of honour should
be conferred upon her :

"The Minister, Li Hungchang, and others, on their
knees memorialise in reply to the Imperial command
made known as follows :—Her late Majesty, Meen-chia-
shun, a lady of perfect virtue and of a family elevated by
its refined breeding, was affianced to His late Majesty,
and became Queen Consort of the 'Central Palace';
her benevolence suffused itself throughout the Court.
The fountain head of the 'female element,' and the first
symbol thus of the earth, she centred around her an
atmosphere of virtue illimitable in extent, and responded
to the divine scheme of nature by co-operating with and
assisting the 'male principle.'

"Her gentleness and excellence formed a pattern for
study, and her strict rectitude exerted influence throughout the six Palaces. Her comportment was retiring and
modest, and for the three years that she graced the Court,

while making manifest the excellence of her rule over
'inner' affairs, she further shared in the anxieties and
toils attending the administration of Government. As
successor to their Majesties the Empresses Dowager, she
further displayed her filial devotion by her attractive and
winning ways; and the many feminine qualities thus
illustriously exhibited have been evident to every inmate
of the Palace. In conformity with the regulations
handed down by our ancestors, it is fitting that a
glorious epitaph and posthumous title be selected for
Her departed Majesty; and the Ministry is hereby commanded to examine and carefully note the records and
ceremonial canons, and to respectfully make a suitable
selection. The Ministers, while paying additional tribute
to the memory of Her departed Majesty, remark with the
greatest humility that where the virtues (of an Emperor
and his Consort) harmonise, the effect may be compared
to the sun and moon beautifying the heavens—[note : the
sun is another emblem of the male and the moon of the
female principle]—and that where the two natures accord,
the female acts in unison with the male and the scheme
of nature is thus carried out. In obedience to the
Imperial command, the Ministers submit two selections
of epitaphs, each twelve characters, and both embodying
the two characters of the deceased Queen's life— title of
Chia-shun—'excellent' and 'yielding.' In reply to the
memorial, the following twelve characters have been
marked out by the vermilion pencil: Hsiao, chê, chia,
shun, shu, shên, hsien, ming, hsien, t'ien changshêng
(I hwang hou). 'Queen I [I, the posthumous term of
the late Emperor], the filial, wise, excellent yielding,
chaste, careful, virtuous, and intelligent, who governed
her actions by the laws of heaven, and whose life added
lustre to the teachings of the sages.'"

CHAPTER VIII.

LI was now high in favour, and was repeatedly summoned to Peking to hold conferences with the Regents. Unhappily, the new reign began badly, so far as foreign relations were concerned. It had been arranged that the Viceroy of India should send an expedition under Colonel Browne, *via* Bhamo in Burma into Yunnan, the south-western province of the empire, and in order to facilitate the passage of the mission through Chinese territory, Mr. Margary, of the China Consular Service, was appointed to meet Colonel Browne at the frontier, and to conduct him and his companions to the conclusion of their journey. Without let or hindrance he travelled across the empire from east to west, and finally reached Bhamo, where he found the members of the expedition awaiting his arrival. By the Chinese officials in the province of Yunnan he had been received with great courtesy, and by none more so than by Li Hsieh-t'ai, an officer whose name was destined to come into unfortunate prominence later on. A most inopportune delay of three weeks occurred while the expedition was

making ready to start from Bhamo, and before they were
well on the road, reports reached them that a Chinese
force was collecting to bar their progress. This was so
contrary to Mr. Margary's experiences on his journey
westward, that he was unwilling to believe in the truth of
the rumour, and with Colonel Browne's consent he went
in advance of the expedition, to pick up what information
he could on the road. On the 19th of February (1875) he
arrived in safety at Manwyne, within the Chinese frontier.
There on the following day he was treacherously murdered,
and simultaneously a large Chinese force marched to the
attack of Colonel Browne's party. These assailants were
driven off without much difficulty, but as an advance
under the circumstances was plainly impossible, Colonel
Browne retreated to Bhamo. So soon as the news of
this outrage reached Peking, Sir Thomas Wade made
vigorous remonstrances at the Tsungli Yamén, and
demanded that a joint commission of English officials
and Chinese mandarins should be appointed to investigate
on the spot the circumstances connected with the outrage.
It will be remembered that only a few months previously
Mr. Wade had, by his kindly intervention, prevented the
outbreak of a disastrous war between Japan and China.
At that time Prince Kung and his colleagues had expressed their gratitude for his mediation in lively terms.
It might have been expected, therefore, that on the present occasion they would have shown every disposition to
meet the British Minister's reasonable demands. This
however was far from being the case. For months they
prevaricated and delayed, on the ground that they had
received no official report of the murder, and although

Sir Thomas Wade supplied them with full particulars of the outrage, they contented themselves with the promulgation of a decree ordering the Governor of Yunnan to enquire into the matter, and desiring Li Hungchang to appoint an officer who should accompany Mr. Grosvenor whom Sir Thomas Wade had determined to send to Yunnan as the English Commissioner. The Viceroy's choice fell on a Taot'ai named Sung, but as the rank of this man was plainly insufficient to carry the necessary weight for so important an investigation, the Government was at length compelled to order Li Hanchang, a brother of the Viceroy, and himself the Viceroy of Hu Kwang, to proceed to Manwyne to hold an enquiry.

Meanwhile Sir Thomas Wade left Peking for Shanghai in order to be within easy telegraphic distance of Downing Street, and at the same time to be able to communicate with Mr. Grosvenor, whom he had sent up the Yangtsze Kiang in the expectation that he could find Li Hanchang ready to start for Yunnan. But that officer was by no means inclined to hurry himself, and the prospect of an early departure westward being plainly past praying for, Mr. Grosvenor returned to his chief, who, there now being less reason for his remaining at Shanghai, left for Tientsin, on his way to the capital. At Tientsin, however, he found Li ready to enter into negotiations with him, and in a memorandum dated August 11th, he informed Li of the very unsatisfactory conduct of his brother, and further put forward five demands which should in his opinion be satisfied by the Chinese Government before any reasonable prospect of securing a satisfactory result could be looked for. First he laid it down:

" If the Chinese Government desires to secure itself and foreign Powers against the dangers of such misunderstandings as that now impending, it would improve the present condition of diplomatic intercourse, beginning, of course, at home, etc.

" Secondly, the Chinese Government will make a serious effort to give effect to the articles of the treaty affecting trade both at the ports and inland. Its present order of proceeding is at some points crippling, at others destroying the trade, not less to the loss of the revenue than to the injury of the foreign merchant. . . .

" Thirdly, the Prince of Kung ought immediately to give me an assurance in writing that such an escort shall be provided for Mr. Grosvenor as will guarantee his safety as far as Manwyne, and, if he desire to return by Rangoon, as far as the point on the frontier nearest Bhamo. . . .

" Fourthly, a similar assurance should be given me regarding the escort of a fresh mission from India. . . .

" Fifthly, the Prince of Kung, as soon as he receives my report of the outrage, should immediately lay it before the Throne, and a decree should be issued requiring the Acting Governor-General Ts'ên to state how it happens that nearly six months after the event no more precise information has been forwarded to Peking than that contained in the memorial of the Acting Governor-General, quoted in the Prince's despatch on 31st July. . . .

" Sixthly, a minister of high rank should at once be sent to England to express the regret of the Chinese Government at what had occurred. . . .

" Seventhly, the decree directing this minister to proceed to England should also appear in the *Gazette*."

These propositions Sir Thomas Wade made it plain were only advanced unofficially, for he rightly held, as he repeatedly took care to impress upon Li, that as British Minister he could only negotiate formally on foreign affairs with the Tsungli Yamên. He, however, found the Viceroy conciliatory in his views, and was gratified to get from

him assurances that he would urge his brother, Li Han-
chang, to lose no time in making a thorough investigation
into the circumstances connected with Margary's murder
and the attack on Colonel Browne's party, and that he
would further advise the Tsungli Yamên to view favourably the propositions advanced in Sir Thomas Wade's
memorandum. In this last respect he was not quite so
successful as his assurances had led Sir Thomas Wade
to expect. With regard to an improvement in diplomatic
relations, the Tsungli Yamên replied that it was not in
accordance with Chinese custom, for Chinese officials who
were not charged with the management of foreign affairs
to hold intercourse with foreigners, "and it consequently
behoves them," they added, "not to be in relations with
the foreign representatives at Peking." The Yamên on
the second point declared themselves ready and willing to
give effect to the articles of the treaty affecting trade.
They promised also, thirdly, to furnish an escort to Mr.
Grosvenor on his journey to Yunnan; and, fourthly, they
further promised to provide an escort for any future
mission which might be sent overland from India to
China. They excused themselves from laying Sir Thomas
Wade's report of the outrage before the Throne, and from
securing the promulgation of an Imperial decree on the
subject, on the ground that it was contrary to Chinese
usage that a decree should be issued until the case in
point was finally settled. As to an envoy being sent to
England, they declared that the subject of sending
ministers to foreign countries had been for some time
under discussion, but that "no suitable persons being
forthcoming for the moment, it had been impossible to

carry it into immediate execution." And that as there was no minister to be sent, no decree on the subject was necessary; and they added "that it is not open to the servants of His Majesty, the Emperor, to make suggestions regarding his decrees."

This memorandum, as well as the general attitude of the Tsungli Yamên, were so very unsatisfactory that Sir Thomas Wade determined to return to Peking to bring his personal influence to bear on the Yamên. On the eve of his departure from Tientsin, however, Li begged him to delay his journey, on the allegation that he had received a copy of a decree which was about to be published, instructing him and a mandarin named Ting to confer with the British minister on the Margary affair with a view to a satisfactory adjustment. A few days later the decree appeared. It was laconic to a degree, and ran as follows, "Let Li Hungchang and Ting Jih-ch'ang negotiate respecting the Margary affair with the British Minister, Mr. Wade, at Tientsin, as he is on the spot, with a view to satisfactory results." The publication of this document, together with the somewhat cavalier assertion in a despatch from Prince Kung, that "he (Sir Thomas Wade) can without hesitation confer and take action with their excellencies Li and Ting," justified the British Minister, as he thought, in opening negotiations with those officials. In the communications which passed Li showed a friendly disposition, and undertook that a memorial should be presented from the Yamên, complaining of the dilatoriness of Ts'ên, the Governor of Yunnan, and that this memorial should appear in the *Peking Gazette*. These concessions the

Yamên promptly refused to endorse, and one of the
Assistant Grand Secretaries took the opportunity of
observing "that it did not follow that what his Excellency
Li might guarantee at Tientsin was to be given effect
to at Peking."

But events proved that the Yamên was not altogether
as inexorable as they at first appeared to be, and on
the 28th of September a decree was issued, which
"enjoined the duty of diplomatic intercourse in very
satisfactory terms." This document having been obtained, Sir Thomas Wade consented to Mr. Grosvenor's
departure for Yunnan, whither Li Hanchang after two
months of leisurely preparation had preceded him.

The way in which the Yamên had declined to sanction
Li's undertakings made it plainly impossible for Sir
Thomas Wade to continue official relations with the
Viceroy. This, however, did not prevent him, as the
negotiations dragged their slow length along, from repeatedly seeing Li, and discussing with him the burning
question of the day. Like all Chinese officials Li has
a very tender regard for Mandarins of the higher ranks.
He would always be ready to sacrifice any number of the
people, and a fair sprinkling of junior officials, if there
was any necessity for it, but he has always shown himself anxious to protect any one enjoying the same or
nearly the same rank as himself. In the matter of the
Margary murder he was prepared to draw the line at
Li Hsieh-t'ai. This officer and any others below him
whom it might be advisable to offer up he was ready
to hand over for punishment, but as to the question
of implicating the Viceroy of Yunnan in the crime, he

would none of it. And even for Li Hsieh-t'ai, he was
anxious to make the best terms he could. He plainly
admitted that he was guilty of having taken part in
the attack on the expedition, but at the same time he
urged on Sir Thomas Wade the advisability of excluding
him from the list of the accused, on the ground that
in case foreign trade were established between Bhamo
and Yunnan, he alone had sufficient influence with
the border tribes to preserve peace and quiet on the
frontier.

If the Tsungli Yamên had honestly supported Li in his
negotiations with Sir Thomas Wade the whole matter
might have been brought to a satisfactory conclusion
in the month of August, 1875. But after having appointed him to conduct the negotiations, they with ease
and apparent indifference threw him over on the very first
occasion which offered. This was but a prelude to a
long series of prevarications, deceptions, and delays on
the part of the Peking authorities. One matter, though
in itself comparatively trifling, was sufficient to indicate
the disposition of the Chinese Government, and to some
extent to call Li's sincerity in question. It will be
remembered that during the T'aip'ing Rebellion, when
the quarrel between Li and Burgevine had reached an
acute stage, a certain mandarin named Sieh was sent
to Peking by Li to represent to the Government his
views on the question in dispute. This man, whom Sir
Frederick Bruce then denounced as a determined foe to
foreigners, and an arch-mischief-maker, was, in spite of
the British Minister's remonstrances, appointed a minister
at the Tsungli Yamên, and had of late years lived in

retirement at his home in Szech'uen. At Li's suggestion,
as it was commonly said, this agitator was now appointed
as colleague to Li Hanchang, in the investigation of the
circumstances connected with the Yunnan outrage. In a
conversation with Sir Thomas Wade at Tientsin, Li had
casually mentioned the appointment of Sieh, but as no
decree had appeared in the *Peking Gazette* on the subject,
Sir Thomas Wade had no direct official evidence on
which to act. Li's information proved, however, to be
correct, but the Government being well aware how
unpopular the appointment would be with the British
Minister, suppressed the decree for five or six months,
and only published it when Sieh had done all the
mischief of which he was capable.

The investigations undertaken in Yunnan were, under
these circumstances, not likely to turn out satisfactorily,
and the British Minister found himself in the undignified
position of being "befooled," as he expressed it in a
despatch to Prince Kung, both by the Yamên and the
Chinese commissioners on the spot. The offers which
were made to punish, now some border tribesmen, now
the local militia, and now some minor officials, were one
and all refused by Sir Thomas Wade, whose sense of
justice was outraged by the indifference with which the
Government proposed to put to death, or otherwise
punish, men whom, as he firmly believed, had nothing
whatever to do with the outrage. He therefore brushed
the question of punishment aside, and emphatically
declared that unless the Yamên were prepared to give the
full redress for the murder of Margary, and the attack on
Colonel Browne's expedition, which he had repeatedly

demanded, he should break off diplomatic relations. This threat having failed to induce the Chinese Government to act in an honourable and straightforward manner, Sir Thomas carried out his resolve, and left Peking for Shanghai.

So much uncertainty had attended the negotiations, and so many propositions and counter-propositions had been advanced by both sides, that it was only that which was determined upon that was unexpected. The news that Sir Thomas Wade had actually left Peking came as a complete surprise to Prince Kung and his colleagues. As in all cases where Chinamen are met with a determined policy, they on this occasion at once tried to recall the action which had produced the crisis. Without the loss of a moment Prince Kung despatched a decree to Li Hungchang, directing him to open negotiations with Sir Thomas at Tientsin on the Margary case. So great had been the haste employed that on Sir Thomas reaching Tientsin a letter from Prince Kung was put into his hands enclosing the decree spoken of, and expressing regret that he had left Peking with such un-Chinese celerity. Acting on the terms of the decree Li, who entered thoroughly into the Prince's diplomacy, invited Sir Thomas to confer with him on the subject in dispute. It is a feature of Chinese diplomatists that they never learn by experience, and never remember anything but what is gratifying to their national pride. Both Prince Kung and Li showed themselves determined to ignore the results of the preceding year, and Li was therefore somewhat taken aback when Sir Thomas declined the invitation, on the ground that only a few months before

the Tsungli Yamén, after having obtained a decree
appointing Li to negotiate on this same subject, had
thrown him over on the first occasion.

Sir Thomas therefore disregarded Li's entreaties, and
proceeded to Shanghai, where he was presently followed
by Mr. Hart, who brought a note from Prince Kung,
as well as an intimation from the Tsungli Yamén, that
if he would consent to meet a special commissioner,
especially appointed to discuss the position with him,
they would be prepared to move the Throne to nominate
one. This offer presented a fair prospect of successful
negotiations, and Sir Thomas intimated that if Li were
appointed to confer with him at Chefoo by the middle of
August he would meet him there. At first it was
proposed by the Chinese Government to nominate Shén,
the Viceroy of the two Kiang provinces, for the office.
Circumstances, however, made this appointment inopportune, and Li Hungchang was ultimately and most
fortunately appointed in his stead.

The idea of going to Chefoo to meet Sir Thomas was,
however, distasteful to Li on several grounds, principally
because he regarded it as derogatory to go to the British
Minister instead of the British Minister coming to him.
A Chinese politician has many ways of attempting to gain
his end, and on this occasion Li set in motion a scheme
which is throughly characteristic of his countrymen. A
hint was given to the notables of Tientsin that Li would
be gratified by their finding an excuse to prevent his
going to Chefoo. At once an agitation was set on foot.
It was declared that the drought which had afflicted
the province for some weeks had disposed the people

to disorder and riot ; that the natives were notoriously a rough and unruly lot ; and that Li was the only man who could hold them well in check. It was feared, therefore, by the leaders of public opinion in Tientsin that if, at this juncture, Li's presence was withdrawn there would probably be a rising, in course of which, it was shrewdly observed, the lives and property of foreigners would be in danger. One of the prime movers in this agitation had rendered himself conspicuous in the riots which had accompanied the Tientsin massacre. It was to be presumed, therefore, that he was well acquainted with the rowdy part of the population, and that he was also unprincipled was shown by the fact that at a later period, when charged with the duty of supplying food to his destitute countrymen during the terrible famine which afflicted the province, he mixed such quantities of alum with the millet which he was charged to distribute, as to check even the appetites of the poor starving applicants, and thus succeeded in filling his own ignoble pocket.

The results of the cogitations of this agitator and his colleagues took the form of the following petition, addressed to Sir Thomas Wade, which was carried by a deputation to Chefoo :

"August 10, 1876.

[Translation.]

" WE, the notables and people of the entire Prefecture of Tien-tsin, in the Empire of China, respectfully present the following petition to your Excellency.

"We humbly submit that we have learnt that his Excellency, the Grand Secretary Li, has received Imperial commands to proceed to Chefoo, for the purpose of negotiating with your Excellency on certain matters. It is publicly bruited abroad that he is to set out on his journey forthwith.

"Whilst, however, we had been informed in the first instance that your Excellency was to arrive at Chefoo immediately, we subsequently heard a report that there had been postponement in this respect, which statement was followed by another to the effect that your Excellency was likely, after all, to be at Chefoo.

"The public mind was at a loss for an explanation; whilst added to this was the fact that the Prefecture of Tien-tsin had been afflicted throughout the spring and summer by a severe drought, entailing deficiency in the crops, and reducing multitudes of the population to want.

"The state of affairs is altogether similar to that which prevailed in consequence of the floods in 1871, and in that year the population of the entire Prefecture owed its salvation to the measures taken by his Excellency Li, in applying to the Throne for sanction to remissions of taxation, and the distribution of relief, by which means scores of thousands were preserved from death.

"At the present moment, the people are famishing in consequence of drought, and there is serious reason to apprehend that at Tien-tsin, a port at which foreigners reside for purposes of trade, the famine-stricken population may commit excesses in the way of plunder, thus entailing injury upon both the Chinese and the foreign mercantile community.

"His Excellency Li being at present engaged in the direction of measures for the repression of disorder and for diffusing tranquility, both foreign and Chinese residents owe their immunity from disturbance to his action.

"Tien-tsin, moreover, is the gateway of access to the capital, and his Excellency Li is one of the pillars of the State, looked up to with veneration by the notables and people of the entire Empire.

"Remembering, as we do in all humility, that relations of friendship have long subsisted between your Excellency's country and the Government of China, and that whenever earnest representations have been made, your Excellency has always deigned to give consent to what has been entreated, for which we, the notables and people of Tientsin, have long cherished feelings of respectful gratitude, we have accordingly determined, after repeated deliberation, to request his Excellency the Envoy-designate Hsü, and the Prefect Ma, to take us with them on the journey we have now undertaken, for the purpose of going with all respect to meet your Excellency, and to invite your Excellency to honour Tien-tsin with a visit.

"If our request be allowed to prevail, his Excellency Li will be enabled to attend at once to the repression of disorder and the diffusion of tranquility, and also to the questions connected with international relations. We, on our part, shall be filled with gratitude without bounds for the consideration shown us by your Excellency.

"It is, of course, our duty to abstain from all interference in the matters forming subject of discussion between your Excellency's Government and our own. With reference to these, we humbly entreat that your Excellency will confer with his Excellency Li."

N. B.—The foregoing paper was presented in the form of a copy of an official document rather than in that of a petition or address. It was accompanied, when handed to the undersigned by the Envoy Hsü, by an envelope containing four slips of red paper, upon which are set forth the names and titles of forty-five of the notables of Tien-tsin. The leading names are as follows:

Hwang She-hi, an expectant Taot'ai.
Wang Wên-yu,　　　,,　　Sub-Prefect.
Yen K'êh-k'wan,　　,,　　Captain.
Wang Pei-keng,　　　,,　　Assistant Magistrate.
　　　&c.,　　　&c.,　　　&c.

(Signed)　　W. F. MAYERS, *Chinese Secretary*.

Sir Thomas Wade not having arrived at Chefoo the deputation was received by Mr. Mayers, the Chinese Secretary of Legation, who informed the members that the following imperial decree having been promulgated

Li could not possibly refuse to obey the commands of
his Imperial Master. "Let the Grand Secretary, Li
Hungchang, Governor-General of Chihli," so ran the
edict, "enter upon the position of High Minister
Plenipotentiary, empowered to take such action as the
circumstances may require, and proceed forthwith to
Yent'ai (Chefoo), for the purpose of conferring in all
matters whatsoever with the British Minister Wei T'oma
(Sir T. Wade)." The notables were at the same time
assured of the peaceful tendency of Li's mission, and
were informed that the fear which they had half expressed
that Li might be held as a hostage was entirely without
foundation.

The British Minister arrived at Chefoo on the 10th of
August, and the negotiations began at once. Sir
Thomas had previously insisted on the necessity of
summoning Ts'ên, the Governor of Yunnan, to Peking,
on the ground that he was virtually responsible for the
Yunnan outrage. He had partly arrived at an estimate
of his guilt, from the truculent disposition of the man.
Ts'ên had been instrumental in suppressing a wide-spread
rebellion in the province, and he had effected this
beneficent result by a series of wholesale massacres, in
which both the guilty and innocent had alike suffered.
Yeh, the Governor of Canton, it may be remembered,
beheaded seventy thousand persons under similar circumstances in 1857. This was barbarous enough, but Ts'ên's
action made Yeh appear in the light of a merciful ruler.
It was impossible to suppose, argued Sir Thomas Wade,
that any subordinate official would have ventured to
lift a finger, much more embroil his country in a possible

foreign war, without having first obtained the sanction of
this merciless Nero. Li met this demand by a counter
proposition, that distinct evidence should first be produced against the governor before taking so strong
a step as summoning him to Peking. Eventually this
claim was given up, and another list of propositions was
tabulated by the British Minister. Sir Thomas was
gratified by the conciliatory attitude of the Chinese
Commissioner, but, as he subsequently wrote to Lord
Derby, "the problem of relations with the foreigner
otherwise than as his superior, is still unsolved by the
majority of Chinese of the class whose education qualifies
them for office : and the conversion, even though it be
but partial, from the exclusivist policy of that majority,
which is the inevitable consequence of an increased
contact with the foreigner, and greater conversance with
the knowledge which gives him power. is still regarded by
it, but as a falling away from the orthodox belief. The
first term that occurs to a Chinese, orthodox in the
above sense, who would describe a progressist of his own
country, as we use the word progressist, is 'renegade'
or 'traitor.' And this appellative has been freely applied
to the Grand Secretary, Li Hungchang, who, though his
larger experience of foreign men and things, especially
men and things of war, has impressed him on behalf of
his country with the necessity of an expansion of her
own ways, if her independency is to be secured, has
neither forgotten his reverence for her history or philo-
sophy, nor is indifferent to any measure that might compromise, however remotely, either her dignity or her
advantage."

On both sides there was a desire to come to terms. The Foreign Office, with that nervous timidity which characterizes our policy in Eastern lands, had given Sir Thomas distinctly to understand that he was not to embroil his Government too deeply with the Tsungli Yamên, and Li being actuated with an equally sincere desire to avoid war was ready to view matters in a friendly spirit. Ts'ên, the governor of Yunnan, had already been degraded by Imperial edict, and Li Sieh-t'ai, with eleven natives who were accused of the actual murder of Margary, had been arrested, and ordered to Yunnan Fu for trial. So far the Tsungli Yamên claimed that they had acted up to the evidence which had been brought before them. According to the report furnished by Li Hanchang, the murder was the act of savages who had demanded blackmail; that Margary had refused to pay it, and had been killed by them in consequence, and that it was at the instigation of Li Sieh-t'ai that Colonel Browne's party had been stopped. In consonance with the Chinese principle of interdependence, Li admitted that the governor of the province shared to a certain extent the crime of these men. Punishment in the shape of degradation having already been meted out to him, there remained in the Viceroy's opinion only the cases of Li Sieh-t'ai and the imprisoned savages. These men he declared that his Government were prepared to prosecute. But Sir Thomas Wade, though willing to believe that Li Sieh-t'ai had been the prime mover in the opposition offered to Colonel Browne, was by no means satisfied that the savages offered up to him had had any share in the murder imputed to them.

He therefore firmly declined to permit the punishment of the prisoners, and sought, by demanding improved official intercourse and additional trading regulations, to put matters on so satisfactory a basis, that such outrages as those of which he had to complain were not likely to recur. Li was by no means averse to treat on this basis, and on the 13th September, 1876, the following convention, known as the Chefu Convention, was signed by Sir T. Wade and Li Hungchang :

"SECTION I. *Settlement of the Yunnan Case.*

"1. A memorial is to be presented to the Throne, whether by the Tsungli Yamên or by the Grand Secretary, Li, is immaterial, in the sense of the memorandum * prepared by Sir Thomas Wade. Before presentation, the Chinese text of the memorial is to be shewn to Sir Thomas Wade.

"2. The memorial having been presented to the Throne, and the Imperial decree in reply received, the Tsungli Yamên will communicate copies of the memorial and Imperial decree to Sir Thomas Wade, together with a copy of a letter from the Tsungli Yamên to the Provincial Governments, instructing them to issue a proclamation that shall embody at length the above memorial and decree. Sir Thomas Wade will thereupon reply to the effect that for two years to come officers will be sent, by the British Minister, to different places in the provinces to see that the proclamation is posted. On application from the British Minister, or the consul of any port instructed by him to make application, the high officers of the provinces will depute competent officers to accompany those so sent to the places which they go to observe.

"3. In order to the framing of such regulations as will be needed for the conduct of the frontier trade between Burma and Yün Nan, the memorial, submitting the pro-

* See p. 133.

posed settlement of the Yün Nan affair, will contain a
request that an Imperial decree be issued, directing the
Governor-General and Governor, whenever the British
Government shall send officers to Yün Nan, to select a
competent officer of rank to confer with them, and to
conclude a satisfactory arrangement.

"4. The British Government will be free for five years,
from the 1st January next, being the 17th day of the 11th
moon of the 2nd year of the reign Kwang Sü, to station
officers at Tali Fu, or at some other suitable place in Yün
Nan, to observe the conditions of trade ; to the end that
they may have information upon which to base the
regulations of trade when these have to be discussed.
For the consideration and adjustment of any matter
affecting British officers or subjects, these officers will be
free to address themselves to the authorities of the province.   The opening of the trade may be proposed by
the British Government, as it may find best, at any time
within five years, or upon expiry of the term of five
years.

" Passports having been obtained last year for a mission
from India into Yün Nan, it is open to the Viceroy
of India to send such mission at any time he may see
fit.

"5. The amount of indemnity to be paid on account
of the families of the officers and others killed in Yün
Nan ; on account of the expenses which the Yün Nan
case has occasioned ; and on account of claims of British
merchants arising out of the action of officers of the
Chinese Government, up to the commencement of the
present year, Sir Thomas Wade takes upon himself to fix
at 200,000 taels, payable on demand.

"6. When the case is closed an Imperial letter will be
written, expressing regret for what has occurred in Yün
Nan.   The mission bearing the Imperial letter will
proceed to England immediately.   Sir Thomas Wade
is to be informed of the constitution of this mission, for
the information of his Government.   The text of the
Imperial letter is also to be communicated to Sir Thomas
Wade by the Tsungli Yamén.

"Section II. *Official Intercourse.*

"Under this heading are included the conditions of intercourse between high officers in the capital and the provinces, and between consular officers and Chinese officials at the ports; also the conduct of judicial proceedings in mixed cases.

"1. In the Tsungli Yamên's memorial of the 28th September, 1875, the Prince of Kung and the ministers stated that their object in presenting it had not been simply the transaction of business in which Chinese and foreigners might be concerned; missions abroad and the question of diplomatic intercourse lay equally within their prayer.

"To the prevention of further misunderstanding upon the subject of intercourse and correspondence, the present conditions of both having caused complaint in the capital and in the provinces, it is agreed that the Tsungli Yamên shall address a circular to the Legations, inviting foreign representatives to consider with them a code of etiquette, to the end that foreign officials in China, whether at the ports or elsewhere, may be treated with the same regard as is shown them when serving abroad in other countries, and as would be shown to Chinese agents so serving abroad.

"The fact that China is about to establish missions and consulates abroad renders an understanding on these points essential.

"2. The British Treaty of 1858, Article XVI., lays down that 'Chinese subjects who may be guilty of any criminal act towards British subjects shall be arrested and punished by Chinese authorities, according to the laws of China.

"'British subjects who may commit any crime in China shall be tried and punished by the consul, or any other public functionary authorized thereto, according to the laws of Great Britain.

"'Justice shall be equitably and impartially administered on both sides.'

"The words 'functionary authorized thereto,' are, translated in the Chinese text, 'British Government.'

"In order to the fulfilment of its treaty obligations, the British Government has established a Supreme Court at Shanghai, with a special code of rules, which it is now about to revise. The Chinese Government has established at Shanghai a Mixed Court, but the officer presiding over it, either from lack of power or dread of unpopularity, constantly fails to enforce his judgments.

"It is now understood that the Tsungli Yamèn will write a circular to the Legations, inviting foreign representatives at once to consider with the Tsungli Yamèn the measures needed for the more effective administration of justice at the ports open to trade.

" 3. It is agreed that, whenever a crime is committed affecting the person or property of a British subject, whether in the interior or at the open ports, the British minister shall be free to send officers to the spot to be present at the investigation.

"To the prevention of misunderstanding on this point, Sir Thomas Wade will write a note to the above effect, to which the Tsungli Yamèn will reply, affirming that this is the course of proceeding to be adhered to for the time to come.

"It is further understood that so long as the laws of the two countries differ from each other, there can be but one principle to guide judicial proceedings in mixed cases in China ; namely, that the case is tried by the official of the defendant's nationality, the official of the plaintiff's nationality merely attending to watch the proceedings in the interests of justice. If the officer so attending be dissatisfied with the proceedings, it will be in his power to protest against them in detail. The law administered will be the law of the nationality of the officer trying the case. This is the meaning of the words '*hui'ung*,' indicating combined action in judicial proceedings, in Article xvi. of the Treaty of Tientsin, and this is the course to be respectively followed by the officers of either nationality.

"Section III. *Trade.*

" 1. With reference to the area within which, according to the Treaties in force, *li-kin* ought not to be collected on foreign goods at the open ports, Sir Thomas Wade agrees to move his Government to allow the ground rented by foreigners (the so-called concessions) at the different ports to be regarded as the area of exemption from *li-kin ;* and the Government of China will thereupon allow I-ch'ang in the province of Hu-Pei, Wu-hei in An-Hui, Wen Chow in Che-kiang, and Pei-hai (Pak-hoi) in Kwang-Tung, to be added to the number of ports open to trade, and to become consular stations. The British Government will farther be free to send officers to reside at Ch'ung-k'ing to watch the conditions of British trade in Ssu-Ch'uen. British merchants will not be allowed to reside at Ch'ung-k'ing, or to open establishments or warehouses there, so long as no steamers have access to the port. When steamers have succeeded in ascending the river so far, further arrangements can be taken into consideration.

" It is farther proposed as a measure of compromise that on certain points on the shore of the Great River ; namely, Ta-t'ung and Ngan-ch'ing, in the province of An-Hui ; Hu-k'ou, in Kiang-Si ; Wu-sueh, Lu-chi-k'ou, and Sha-shih, in Hu-Kuang—these being all places of trade in the interior, at which, as they are not open ports, foreign merchants are not legally authorized to land or ship goods—steamers shall be allowed to touch for the purpose of landing or shipping passengers or goods ; but in all instances by means of native boats only, and subject to the regulations affecting native trade.

" Produce accompanied by a half-duty certificate may be shipped at such points by the steamers, but may not be landed by them for sale. And at all such points, except in the case of imports accompanied by a transit duty certificate, or exports similarly certificated, which will be severally passed free of *li-kin* on exhibition of such certificates, *li-kin* will be duly collected on all goods whatever by the native authorities. Foreign merchants will not be authorized to reside or open houses of business or warehouses at the places enumerated as ports of call.

"2. At all ports open to trade, whether by earlier or later agreement, at which no settlement area has been previously defined, it will be the duty of the British Consul, acting in concert with his colleagues, the Consuls of other Powers, to come to an understanding with the local authorities regarding the definition of the foreign settlement area.

"3. On opium, Sir Thomas Wade will move his Government to sanction an arrangement different from that affecting other imports. British merchants, when opium is brought into port, will be obliged to have it taken cognizance of by the Customs, and deposited in bond, either in a warehouse or a receiving hulk, until such time as there is a sale for it. The importer will then pay the tariff duty upon it, and the purchasers the *li-kin;* in order to the prevention of the evasion of the duty, the amount of *li-kin* to be collected will be decided by the different provincial governments, according to the circumstances of each.

"4. The Chinese Government agrees that transit duty certificates shall be framed under one rule at all ports, no difference being made in the conditions set forth therein ; and that so far as imports are concerned, the nationality of the person possessing and carrying these is immaterial. Native produce carried from an inland centre to a port of shipment, if *bonâ-fide* intended for shipment to a foreign port may be, by Treaty, certificated by the British subject interested, and exempted by payment of the half duty from all charges demanded upon it *en route.* If produce be not the property of a British subject, or is being carried to a port not for exportation, it is not entitled to the exemption that would be secured it by the exhibition of a transit duty certificate. The British Minister is prepared to agree with the Tsung-li Yamên upon rules that will secure the Chinese Government against abuse of the privilege as affecting produce.

"The word '*nei ti*,' inland, in the clause of Article VII. of the rules appended to the Tariff, regarding carriage of imports inland, and of native produce purchased inland, apply as much to places on the sea coasts and river shores, as to places in the interior not open to foreign trade; the Chinese Government having the right to make arrangements for the prevention of abuses thereat.

"5. Article XLV. of the Treaty of 1858 prescribes no limit to the term within which a drawback may be claimed upon duty-paid imports. The British Minister agrees to a term of three years, after expiry of which no drawback shall be claimed.

"6. The foregoing stipulation, that certain ports are to be opened to foreign trade, and that landing and shipping of goods at six places on the Great River is to be sanctioned, shall be given effect to within six months after receipt of the Imperial decree approving the memorial of the Grand Secretary Li. The date for giving the effect to the stipulations affecting exemption of imports from *li-kin* taxation within the foreign settlements, and the collection of *li-kin* upon opium by the Customs Inspectorate at the same time as the Tariff duty upon it, will be fixed as soon as the British Government has arrived at an understanding on the subject with other foreign Governments.

"7. The Governor of Hong Kong having long complained of the interference of the Canton Customs revenue cruisers with the junk trade of that Colony, the Chinese Government agrees to the appointment of a Commission, to consist of a British Consul, an officer of the Hong Kong Government, and a Chinese official of equal rank, in order to the establishment of some system that shall enable the Chinese Government to protect its revenue without prejudice to the interests of the Colony.

" *Separate Article.*

"Her Majesty's Government having in contemplation to send a mission of exploration next year by way of Peking through Kan-Su and Koko-Nor, or by way of

Ssu-Ch'uen to Thibet, and thence to India, the Tsung-li Yamén, having due regard to the circumstances, will, when the time arrives, issue the necessary passports, and will address letters to the high provincial authorites and to the Resident in Thibet. If the mission should not be sent by these routes, but should be proceeding across the Indian frontier to Thibet, the Tsung-li Yamén, on receipt of a communication to the above effect from the British Minister, will write to the Chinese Resident in Thibet, and the Resident, with due regard to the circumstances, will send officers to take due care of the mission; and passports for the mission will be issued by the Tsung-li Yamén, that its passage be not obstructed.

"Done at Chefoo, in the Province of Shan-Tung, this thirteenth day of September, in the year of our Lord one thousand eight hundred and seventy-six.

> (L.S.) "THOMAS FRANCIS WADE.
> (L.S.) "CHINESE PLENIPOTENTIARY."

Before the signatures were actually affixed to this document, Li received a letter from Sir Thomas Wade, informing him that, in recognition of the frankness with which he had negotiated this very troublesome business, Sir Thomas was prepared to make a distinct concession. Li had previously been given to understand that, on the conclusion of the Convention, the British Government would be asked to consider the case closed. He now learnt that Sir Thomas was willing, on his own responsibility, in case the guarantees he demanded were granted, to declare the Yunnan affair finally settled. With ready despatch Li reported the conclusion of the negotiations to the Throne in a memorial, which was published in the *Peking Gazette.* In this state paper he recapitulated the course which events had taken; explained the unwillingness of Sir Thomas Wade to see the prisoners who had been arrested in Yunnan punished for the crime of which they were accused; and urged on the Emperor the advisability of cementing the friendship of foreign countries, by showing an earnest desire to prevent the possibility of the occurrence of such tragedies in the future.

The uncertainty which had surrounded the negotiations of the case from the beginning, made Li doubly anxious that it should now be definitely closed. He was well aware that it was within the bounds of possibility that the British Government might still demand the punishment of the inculpated officials, and he saw that the best way to avert this was for the Tsungli Yamen to act at once upon the conditions of the Convention. With as little delay as possible the memorials and decrees agreed upon were duly published in the *Peking Gazette;* the opening of the additional ports to trade was proclaimed; the regulations with regard to the *li-kin* tax were promulgated; and the despatch of the newly-appointed minister, Kwo Sungtao, to England, with a letter of apology, was announced. As the departure of this mission marks a new era in our relations with the Flowery Land, we give at length the letter which Kwo carried for presentation to Her Majesty:

"*Letter of Apology from the Emperor of China, and Credentials of the Envoy Kwo Sung-tao, on his Mission to Great Britain, dated October,* 1876.

" (Translation.)

" "THE Emperor of China salutes the Queen of England and Empress of India.

" "Having become inheritor of the great estate by the mandate of heaven, and reverently continued the succes-

sion to our great estate, we have borne in affectionate
remembrance the States in amity with us, and [have
desired] to consolidate for ever relations of friendship
and concord.

"In the first moon of the first year of the reign Kwang
Sü (February, 1875), the official interpreter of your
Majesty's Government, Ma Kia-li (Mr. Margary) by name,
whilst travelling under passport from Burmah, and on
having reached the frontier region of the province of
Yünnan, was murdered, and his companion, Colonel
Browne, was attacked and driven back.

"We made special appointment of Li Han-Chang,
Governor-General of the Hu Kwang provinces, to proceed
to Yünnan for the purpose of instituting inquiry and
taking action in conformity with the principles of justice;
and we furthermore issued a decree, enjoining upon the
Governors-General and Governors of all the provinces
that they should give instructions to all local authorities
within their jurisdiction, to the effect that the provisions
of the treaties must be duly fulfilled, with reference to
all persons travelling under passport in the places under
their authority.

"Li Han-chang, having completed his investigation,
memorialised us, requesting that the military officer Li
Chên-kwoh and others might be severally punished for
their offences.

"In the month of August last, we further specially
appointed Li Hung-chang, a Senior Grand Secretary,
Governor-General of the province of Chihli, of the first
class of the Third Order of Nobility, to proceed as High
Minister Plenipotentiary to Chefoo, in the province of
Shantung, to act there with your Majesty's Special Envoy
Wei Toma (Sir Thomas Wade) in arranging the terms of
a settlement of this case. Li Hung-chang has memorialised us, in reply, stating that your Majesty's Envoy, Sir
Thomas Wade, had expressed the opinion that security
for the future was to be preferred to punishment of the
past; and we issued hereupon a special rescript in reply,
according to the request that was made, granting, as an
act of grace, remission of the penalties that had been

incurred by Li Chên-kwoh and the others involved with him, and still further enjoining upon the high authorities of all the provinces implicit obedience to the commands of last year, that protection should be afforded in conformity with the treaty stipulations. We have also commanded the Yamên of Foreign Affairs to draw up a proclamation, and to forward a copy of the draft to each Provincial Government to be acted upon, to the end that tranquillity may prevail in the relations between China and foreigners.

"That Mr. Margary, whilst travelling under passport within the frontier of Yünnan, should have lamentably been murdered, is a fact which not alone involves the question of a loss of life, but which also has gone near to disturb our relations of amity and concord. We profoundly regret and lament it. We have now made special appointment of Kwoh Sung-tao, an acting Senior Vice-President of the Board of Ceremonies, and one of the Ministers of the Office of Foreign Affairs, as Envoy Extraordinary, to proceed to your Majesty's country to give utterance, on our behalf, to the sentiments we have at heart, as a proof of our genuine desire for amity and concord.

" We know Kwoh Sung-tao to be an officer of capacity and experience, of loyalty and truthfulness, who is in disposition amicable and just, and far-reaching in intelligence. He has acquired great familiarity in the treatment of affairs between Chinese and foreign Powers. We would ask that sincere confidence be reposed in him, to the end that the blessings of friendly concord may for ever be experienced in the highest degree, and that all alike may enjoy the happiness of a state of peace. This, we doubt not, will be greatly to the satisfaction [of your Majesty]."

CHAPTER IX.

THE publication of the terms of the Chefoo Convention aroused considerable discussion among British merchants, both in China and in England, and many of its conditions were severely criticised. That it did not entirely meet with the approval of the Foreign Office, was plain from the very marked disinclination which was shown to ratify it. By Li's action, however, it became extremely difficult for the British Government to disown its provisions, though it was not until 1888 that it in part received the official sanction of the British Government.

So far as Li was concerned, however, his object was gained when the Convention was signed, and having entertained Sir Thomas Wade at a farewell dinner, he returned with all speed to Tientsin. It chanced that about this time there was held, according to Chinese custom, a triennial examination of the administration of the civil Mandarins of the province, and advantage was taken of this opportunity to confer further blushing honours on Li Hungchang for his success at Chefoo.

Foreign affairs no longer occupying the greater part of his time, Li had now leisure to devote himself to the administration of his province. True to the policy he had always adopted of adding strength to the military forces under his command, he urged on the completion of the fortifications between Taku and Tientsin, and was before long able to report their completion to the Throne. In his memorial on this subject, he stated that ten thousand soldiers had been employed for three years in the construction of the forts; that the men had agreed to a reduction in their pay to the amount of 500,000 taels for the purchase of materials; and that, therefore, the work had not entailed any cost on the Imperial Government. It must have occurred to most readers of this memorial, that if the statements it contained were strictly in accordance with truth, the leopards must have changed their spots, and the soldiers employed must have been of quite another type from that of the men ordinarily found under Chinese banners. But events seemed to show that Li had been misled as to the self-denying and patriotic conduct of his regiments, for shortly afterwards a revolt broke out among these very men, who complained of having been overworked, and of having had undue reductions made from their pay. Fortunately news of the intended revolt was brought to Li in time to suppress the worst consequences. Out of the 9,000 intending mutineers, however, 3,000 broke out into open revolt and marched away, carrying their arms with them. Li instantly despatched troops, on whom he could rely, in pursuit of the deserters, many of whom were shot down, and the others, with few exceptions, were taken prisoners.

These men were not the *elite* of Li's forces. They were the ordinary Chinese troops, armed with the native gingalls, and fit only to do hard manual labour, or to serve as food for powder. On his own bodyguard, on the other hand, he bestowed considerable attention, arming them with the newest weapons of destruction, and on one occasion nearly met his death from the inexperience of his troops in the use of the new ammunition. A battery of Horse Artillery, armed with Krupp guns, happened to be manœuvring before the Viceroy, when a furious duststorm arose, which drove him to the shelter of a neighbouring shed, near which were stored a number of explosives. By some accident, just as he had seated himself, several of the shells exploded, and with such violence, that six men were blown to atoms, and some forty others were injured. It seems difficult to teach Chinamen the necessity of precaution against fire in the neighbourhood of gun-powder, and Li had his full share of accidents of this kind to report to the Throne. On one occasion a fire broke out at a military store at Tientsin, by which a number of people lost their lives. Li informed his Imperial Master, though without giving any evidence of the fact, that the fire had been caused by spontaneous combustion, and recommended, on the curious Chinese principle of interdependence, that the officer in charge being responsible for the calamity, should be degraded and lose his button. The recommendation was adopted, and the anomalous result followed—that the man was

punished for having permitted the existence of spontaneous combustion.

But though Li considered that the land defences at
Tientsin were placed by his reforms in a satisfactory
condition, he felt the importance of making provisions
for the defence of the water way to that city. With this
object he established a torpedo college at Tientsin, where
sailors were taught the use of this weapon of destruction.
In April, 1877, Li held his first annual inspection of this
establishment, and went through the workshops, inspecting minutely the machinery employed. A number of
torpedoes were then fired off in the river in the neighbourhood of his Yamên, much to the delight of an
immense crowd of spectators, who lined the banks, and
who were well content to get a good sprinkling of the
spray thrown up, in return for the novel and wondrous
sight provided for them. The Viceroy finally presided at
the examination of the youths in technical knowledge and
foreign languages, of both of which subjects, it is needless to say, he was absolutely ignorant, and was therefore
entirely dependent on the reports of the European
Professors as to the efficiency of their pupils. Having
rewarded with prizes the most deserving of the students,
he returned to his Yamên, after a day's work of unwonted
physical exertion. The expense and trouble which he
has devoted to this branch of the service deserves better
results than those given during the late war. Not a single
Japanese ship was injured by the torpedoes which had
cost the great Viceroy so much, and if any evidence of
the non-aggressive spirit of Chinamen were needed, it
might be furnished by the failure of the torpedo service

in the recent campaign. During the war with France,
the same hesitation to employ torpedoes was displayed,
and when a European officer in charge of the boats
made a proposal to blow up the French ships lying at
anchor in the port of Ningpo, the mandarin in command
refused to sanction the venture.

Li's attention, however, was by no means entirely
directed to the development of the Army and Navy.
He was well aware, that in order to strengthen the
country, its resources should be developed, and he was
already beginning to watch with curiosity and some
concern the rapid strides which the Japanese were
making in advancing their country's commercial prosperity. Already the facile islanders had adopted
European machinery for working their mines, and Li
appointed a commission to examine and report on the
system adopted in the land of the Rising Sun. After
mature consideration of the information thus acquired,
Li proposed to form a company, with a capital of 800,000
taels, to work the coal mines in the Metropolitan
Province. The adoption of this step led to the construction of the first *bonâ-fide* railway in China. The
European manager of the mines, knowing the advantages
to be derived from a railway, and being wise in his
generation, gradually led up to a line by the modest
introduction of a tramway, thus familiarising the people
with the sight of rails and railway carriages. About the
same time an injudiciously-managed attempt to foist on
the Chinese a short ready-made railway from Shanghai
to the port of Woosung, met with disaster. It was
abundantly shown that the people were well disposed

towards the enterprise, and Li, who was afterwards consulted in the matter, looked favourably upon it. But the local officials and the Literati had to be consulted, and these waged so successful a war against the line, that although the Viceroy of the two Kiangs had given his consent to its construction, the rails were, after a short season of prosperity, pulled up and transferred to Formosa, where they were allowed to rot on the sea-shore. A better fortune attended Li's enterprise. The country through which it ran—from the mines to Tient-sin—is a thinly-populated and barren district. The chartered opponents of such enterprises, that is, the Literati, were non-existent, and Li's personal influence was sufficient to gain security for the innovation. By degrees the railway, which was at first only used for the conveyance of coal, developed a passenger traffic, and was eventually extended for military purposes to Shanghai Kwan, the point where the great wall reaches the coast. It was the possession of this railway which was demanded by the Japanese, prior to the attempt to assassinate Li, as a condition of granting an armistice, and thus a kind of colour has been given to a doctrine current in China, and which has lately been officially expounded by a censor, to the effect that a railway in the neighbourhood of the coast is dangerous, as it enables an invader to gain ready access to the interior of the country.

If Li had been all powerful he would have applied the same manner of working as that adopted at the coal mines in Chihli to mines throughout the empire. But by the decentralised system of government existing in the country, it is impossible to establish any uniform system in the various provinces, and Li was obliged to turn his attention to other schemes. A telegraph already connected his Yamên with the arsenal, and he gave directions for the erection of posts to connect Taku with Tientsin. As already noticed, he had promoted the establishment of a China Merchants' Steam Navigation Company, which he hoped might compete successfully with the foreign-owned steamers trading along the coast. At first, by the careful employment of official influence to promote its welfare, the scheme answered tolerably well, and in 1877 the Company was in a position to buy the steamers of the Shanghai Steam Navigation Company, with all the dockyard plant, for the sum of 2,000,000 taels. It is amusing to see the efforts which were made by Li to bolster up a concern, which without such aid must have been inevitably ruined by the official element in the management. Unhappily in China the presence of Mandarins on a Board means that bribery and corruption form part of the policy of the undertaking, and this Company, which if left to the hands of mercantile men might have succeeded well, was constantly imperilled by the very support which was intended to give it life and strength. With the plant of the Shanghai Steam Navigation Company, were transferred also the services of the shipping coolies, who, to their dismay, found that under their new masters their wages, which used to be paid them with refreshing regularity and entirety by their European employers, suffered serious diminution before reaching their hands. Like English dockers, Chinese coolies are accustomed to strikes, and they came out in a body at the infliction of this injustice. The iniquity of the proceeding was too plain to be denied, and for the future the official peculators had to look elsewhere for this portion of their ill-gotten gains.

Of this company Li was a most energetic supporter, and never missed an opportunity of throwing freights and business into its hands. In one memorial he reported to the throne that great and manifold advantages would result from carrying the copper produced from the mines in Yunnan by the company's steamers instead of as heretofore by the Grand Canal. In this, as in most matters, he gained his point. But the transfer of the carriage from native craft to the company's steamers did not mitigate all the evils attending the transportation of the copper. The Mint officials at Pekin had loud complaints to make of the delay which occurred in bringing the metal to the capital. So great was the loss of time on one occasion that Li was ordered to make strict enquiry into the matter. Whether he was really so surprised at the result of his investigations as he appeared to be in his report to the Throne, may well be doubted. But at all events he acted the part to perfection, and vigorously denounced the guilty parties. It is well known that precious metals passing through the gates of Peking suffer considerably from shrinkage, and the result of Li's enquiries went to show that the Mint officials were in the habit of regularly levying a tax of 100 taels per 10,000 catties of copper. In this particular instance the consignment had consisted of 500,000 catties, and the tax demanded therefore amounted to 5000 taels, or about £1000. As the official charged with the carriage of the copper had been unable to pay this sum down on the nail, a delay in the delivery had occurred, and matters were just about to be expedited by a suggestion from the Mint authorities that the mandarin in charge should sell a sufficient quantity of the copper to meet the demand, when Li's investigation opened. Having been foolish enough to be found out, the officials concerned were ruthlessly held up to execration, and were handed over to the Board of Punishments for sentence.

In 1877 a tragic misfortune befell the country, which Li strove loyally to mitigate, but which, at the same time, he incidentally succeeded in turning to the advantage of the company. Over a large portion of Northern China there lies a thick deposit of loess—a light and friable soil which is extremely fertile when watered by temperate rains, but which in dry seasons leaves the seeds exposed to the sterilising influence of sun and wind. A rainless season, therefore, means the destruction of the crops, and such seasons occurred in 1877 and 1878. Over the Provinces of Chihli, Shanse, Honan, and parts of Kansuh the crops in each year failed entirely, and the people were left destitute of their natural food. For some time they lived on the leaves and bark of trees, and any roots that they could find, and when these wretched means of sustenance failed, the people for the most part lay down to die. From first to last it was reckoned that about 9,000,000 perished in the course of the famine. As in all great national disasters in China, the Government did all that they were capable of doing to help the distressed. But the means of transport were so bad, and so long a time was allowed to elapse before effective steps were taken, that the worse was over before the Government rice

reached, at all events, the more remote of the afflicted
districts. The Government had no stores of grain on
hand, the supply of food had to be imported, and Li at
once seized the opportunity to recommend that all grain
from the south should be carried in the ships of the
China Merchants' Steam Navigation Company. This
was done, and the supplies unquestionably arrived earlier
than they would have done by the old system of carriage
by junk. But the waste of money in this as in other
respects was very great. Peculation was rife, and some
of Li's subordinates were publicly charged with gross
frauds, in connection with the purchase and distribution
of the grain.

Such men were vehemently denounced by Li, who
used his very best endeavours to relieve the distress, and
to collect funds to purchase the required food. In
December, 1877, he reported that he had received in
donation 289,394 taels, and he memoralized exhaustively
on the best and cheapest markets in which to buy grain.
In the first instance he applied to Japan, but found that
the freights from that country were too heavy. He
therefore directed the Steam Ships Company's agents at
Saigon and the ports of Southern China to procure the
necessary supplies. With indefatigable diligence he
superintended the system of distribution, and effected as
much good as was possible with the appliances at his
command. The superstitious side of Li's nature always
appears on such occasions, and seems to be so completely
opposed to his strong common-sense, that one is tempted
to regard his professed belief in the powers of the
animalistic deities as assumed for the occasion. During

the months of this great drought he frequently besought
the Dragon King to pour water on the thirsty earth, and,
in obedience to an Imperial decree, he brought from
Hantan Hsien a mystic iron tablet, which stands in one
of the temples of that city, and which is said to possess
the power of attracting rain to any district into which it
is carried.   In his anxiety for the welfare of the Imperial
domain, the Emperor desired to have this talisman
transported to Peking, and Li, who, as he wrote, "Was
filled with admiration beyond expression for the solicitude
so unceasingly displayed by His Majesty for the welfare
of his people," hastened to obey the Imperial will.   By
all accounts the results were most satisfactory.   Rain fell,
and the tablet was carried back to Hantan amid adulation
and thanksgivings.

But Li desired also to employ other and more mundane
means for relieving the wants of the people.   He urged
on his Imperial master the advisibility of prohibiting
all distilling until the evil was overpast.   He reckoned
the quantity of grain employed by the distillers, and
calculated that food stuff so used would sustain the lives
of many thousands of those who were then starving.
He opened soup kitchens at Tientsin ; and is said to
have fed a thousand refugees daily from his own purse.
At the same time he had constantly to report to the
Throne the receipt of munificent contributions towards
the relief of the sufferers.   One Peking tea merchant
maintained, at his own cost, two soup kitchens, where
thousands were kept alive daily, and, in addition, contributed 2,000 taels to Li's fund.   The Viceroy's energy
and resource were unbounded in the cause ; and in his

efforts to secure funds he overstepped the bounds of the Empire, and appealed to those countries to which his countrymen mostly emigrate. From Singapore, from Australia, and from California, funds came pouring in. From the Chinese provinces it was reckoned, by a careful computation, that 2,623,644 taels were received. But this sum did not, by any means, include all the amounts gathered even in China itself. The Protestant missionaries in the afflicted districts worked with a zeal and devotion which was beyond all praise, and were loyally supported by the foreign residents at the ports. 7,620 taels were distributed through these voluntary helpers, and a further sum, which was collected in England, was placed at the disposal of the same agencies. The scenes witnessed by these emissaries of mercy were piteous in the extreme. The people, blackened by want, ate ravenously anything which by any chance contained the smallest degree of nourishment; and when all other food failed, they even devoured the corpses of those who had perished before them. Fortunately, it has not often happened in the history of the Empire that such dire disasters have occurred, and well would it have been if the occasion had been seized to improve the existing means of communication between the various provinces. But the necessity for such popular reforms does not appeal to Chinamen. The repairing of the Imperial roads is a different matter; and while the grain carts were yet ploughing their way through the execrable roads which connect Shansi and Honan with Chihli, Li received orders to supply 16,000 taels for the repair of the road from Peking to the Imperial Mausolea, where the remains of the still unburied Emperor and Empress were to be laid.

On all sides Li was called upon at this period to contribute to the Imperial necessities. Almost at the same time as the above demand was made upon him, an edict was issued, ordering him to pay in at once 20,000 taels to the Imperial Equipage Department. But with all these outgoings, he still contrived to find money enough to buy guns and gunboats for the protection of the capital. A fleet of gunboats, named after the first few letters of the Greek alphabet, were added to the ships under his command, and, at his request, the British admiral lent an instructor to teach the native artillery-men the unaccustomed art of naval gunnery.

In a conversation with the admiral, Li asked how many gunboats would it take to engage an ironclad on equal terms.

"Four," replied the admiral, who added, laughing, "but mind, it mustn't be an English ironclad."

"That will never be," was the diplomatic rejoinder; "the friendship between England and China is too genuine to be lightly broken."

The gunboats answered every expectation; but matters did not always go so smoothly with Li's armaments. At an inspection, held about this time, of the Torpedo College, the torpedoes, though laid with the greatest care, one and all declined to explode.

Li was greatly annoyed at this fiasco, and incontinently dismissed the foreign instructor. Europeans taking service under Chinese mandarins are liable to such sudden displacements, even though, as in this case, no fault attaches to the officer in question. Years before, at Nanking, when a similar display was to have been made at the Arsenal, under Dr. Macartney's charge, the doctor was warned by a friendly native that the connections between the batteries and the torpedoes, which had been carefully laid in the bed of the river, in preparation for the inspection, had been cut by a Chinaman who was jealous of the doctor's repute, and very possibly the same motive led, with, however, more unkind result, to the disaster at Tientsin.

Events shortly occurred which seemed plainly to indicate that Li's warlike preparations would be put to the test. It will be remembered that, some nine or ten years previously, Kashgaria had been snatched from China by a successful revolt among the Tungani. The disorder produced by this outbreak spread to the Chinese province of Kuldja, which adjoined Russian territory; and so great was the spirit of unrest in this district, that the Russian Government felt called upon to occupy the province. With due regard for the susceptibilities of China, they announced the fact to the Tsungli Yamèn, and assured that body that as soon as they were in a position to occupy the province in sufficient force to preserve order, it should be at once restored to them. As a result of the successful conclusion of Tso Tsungt'ang's campaign, conducted in the leisurely manner already referred to, the Chinese were in 1878 prepared and ready to garrison effectively the appropriated province Notice was therefore given to the Russian Government, who were, at the same time, requested to act up to their promise. Though no positive objection was raised to

this demand, the Tzar's advisers allowed it to be understood that certain collateral questions would have to be
discussed before the transfer could be made.

On receiving this intimation the Chinese Government
appointed Chung How, who had preceded Li in the office
of Superintendent of Trade for the Northern Ports, to
proceed to St. Petersburg to arrange for the rendition
of the province. After protracted negotiations, caused
partly by the Tzar's visits to Livadia, Chung How
concluded a treaty by the terms of which only part of
the province of Kuldja was to be restored to China,
while the valley of the Tekkes, and the famous military
road leading by the Muzart pass through the Tienshan
range into Kashgaria, were to remain in the hands of
Russia. In addition to this concession, Chung How
agreed that his Government should pay 5,000,000 metal
roubles as an indemnity for the cost of the occupation.
Chung How, like most Chinamen, had little knowledge
of geography or military topography, and he was no
match for the Russians in this part of the negotiations.
Perhaps we ought not to throw stones at the Chinese on
this account, since it is well known that when, some years
ago, a Russian negotiator came to London to discuss the
Khiva question, it was with some difficulty that the then
Secretary of State for Foreign Affairs could find the
district in dispute on the Foreign Office maps. On the
money question, Chung How was fully alive, and made
what must be considered a very good bargain.

Having despatched a copy of the treaty to Peking, the
Ambassador wrote to announce his departure from St.
Petersburg on his homeward journey. On landing at

Shanghai he was received by the native officials with all
honour, and proceeded overland to Peking in state. On
the day of his arrival in the capital, however, there
appeared, to the surprise of most people, an Imperial
decree, handing the Ambassador over to the Board of
Civil Office, for trial and punishment, on the charge of
having returned to China without the special order or
permission of the Emperor. By the same decree, a
Council, consisting of the highest officials in the State,
including Li Hungchang, was appointed to report
collectively and separately, on the new treaty. Amongst
others Li reported adversely of the terms proposed. The
idea of giving up territory is abhorrent to a Chinese
Minister, who regards the Empire as a sacred trust which
has been committed to his keeping for transmission to
the generations yet to come.

It is well known that at this time there had grown up
in the capital a strong war party, headed by Prince Ch'un,
the father of the Emperor, and Tso Tsungt'ang, the hero
of Kashgaria. This clique was directly opposed to the
advocates of Peace, who were represented in the Government by Prince Kung and Li Hungchang. Chung How
was a relative of Prince Kung, and this fact may have
influenced the Prince to a certain extent, but quite
independently of any such consideration, he set himself
in alliance with Li to oppose any step which might
precipitate a war, although at the same time, he cordially
agreed with his colleague in condemning the terms of the
treaty. But Chung How's enemies were powerful and
determined, and in little more than three weeks after his
return to the capital the following decree was issued :

"The Board of Civil Office memorialise that having, in obedience to Imperial command, determined a severe penalty, they beg that Chung How, senior Vice-President of the Board of Censors, may be dismissed the public service in conformity with the law which provides this penalty for offences against the constitution. The circumstances under which Chung How, who was honoured with our commands to go forth on a mission, took upon himself to start on his return without waiting for the Imperial permission to do so, are very grave, and the mere bestowal of dismissal upon him is insufficient to expiate the crime of which he has been guilty. Let him, as a preliminary step, be cashiered and arrested, and, after having been put to the question, let him be handed over to the Board of Punishments for correction."

The Board of Punishments, after due consideration, took a very grave view of Chung How's offence, and as the result of their finding, a decree was issued ordering his decapitation in the autumn.

Having thus successfully attacked Chung How, Prince Ch'un and his confrères turned their attention to Li Hungchang. It is a well-known habit in the East, as was pointed out by Macaulay, that a statesman no sooner falls into disgrace, than clouds of witnesses come forward who are prepared to charge him with crimes of every kind. So it was in Li's case. The Censors vied with one another in bringing accusations against him, and in reply to his declaration that the country was not prepared for war, they demanded what was the use of the vessels and armaments on which he had lavished such vast sums, if, when the country demanded it, they were not available. The position was a particularly trying one for Li. He was from conviction compelled to take the apparently unpatriotic course of advocating concessions to Russia, and he had to meet a powerful and high-placed opposition in Peking. With unfaltering courage he faced his enemies, feeling secure in the fact that he was the only man who was capable of offering a formidable opposition to an invading army. Fortunately for him, however, at this juncture, Colonel Gordon, who had accompanied Lord Ripon to India as his private secretary, accepted Li's invitation to pay him a visit at Tientsin. Gordon's name had become a household word in China, and his advice could not but be received with consideration even by the most heated partizan. On arriving at Tientsin he, in his usually outspoken manner, proclaimed the weakness of the forts and ships on the coast, and the imperfect organisation of the army, and warned Li that a declaration of war would be followed by an invasion of Manchuria, and that a Russian army might be expected before the gates of Pekin within a couple of months from the outbreak of hostilities. At Peking, whither he went at the invitation of the Tsungli-Yamen, he expressed the same matter-of-fact views, and was a powerful factor in the interests of peace. Before taking leave of Li he left in his hands the following memorandum, which, if not on all points wise in the light of recent experiences, was wisdom itself compared to the foolishness of the Chinese :

"China possesses a long-used military organization, a regular military discipline. Leave it intact. It is suited to her people.

"China in her numbers has the advantage over other Powers. Her people are inured to hardships. Arm with breech-loaders, accustom to the use and care of breech-loaders, and no more is needed for her infantry. Breech-loaders ought to be bought on some system, and the same general system applicable to the whole nation. It is not advisable to manufacture them; though means of repair should be established at certain centres.

"Breech-loading ammunition should be manufactuted at different centres. Breech-loaders of various patterns should not be bought, though no objection could be offered to a different breech-loader in, say, four provinces from that used in another group of four provinces. Any breech-loaders which will carry well up to 1000 yards would be sufficient. It is not advisable to spend money on the superior breech-loaders carrying farther. Ten breech-loaders, carrying up to 1000 yards, could be bought for the same money as five breech-loaders of a superior class, carrying to 1500 yards. For the Chinese it would cost more time to teach the use of the longer-range rifle than it is worth; and then probably, if called to use it, in confusion the scholar would forget his lesson. This is known to be the case; therefore buy ordinary breech-loading rifles of 1000 yards range, of simple con-struction, and solid form. Do not go into purchasing a very light, delicately-made rifle. A Chinese soldier does not mind one or two pounds more weight, for he carries no knapsack or kit. China's power is in her numbers, in the quick moving of her troops, in the little baggage they require, in their few wants. It is known that men armed with sword and spear can overcome the best regular troops, if armed with the best breech-loading rifles and well instructed in every way, if the country is at all difficult, and if the men with the spears and swords out-number their foe ten to one. If this is the case when men are armed with spears and swords, it will be much truer when the same are armed with ordinary breech-loaders.

"China should never engage in pitched battles. Her strength is in quick movements, in cutting off the trains of baggage, and in night attacks not pushed home; in a continuous worrying of her enemies. Rockets should be used instead of cannon. No artillery should be moved with the troops. It delays and impedes them. Infantry fire is the most fatal fire; guns make a noise far out of proportion to their value in war. If guns are taken into the field, troops cannot march faster than those guns. The degree of speed at which the guns can be carried along dictates the speed at which the troops can march. Therefore very few guns, if any, ought to be taken; and those few should be smooth-bored, large-bore breech-loaders, consisting of four parts, to be screwed together when needed for use. Chinese accustomed to make forts of earth ought to continue this, and study the use of trenches for the attack of cities. China should never attack forts. She ought to wait and starve her foes out, and worry them night and day. China should have a few small-bored very long range wall-pieces, rifled and breech-loaders. They are light to carry, and if placed a long way off will be safe from attack. If the enemy comes out to take them, the Chinese can run away; and if the enemy takes one or two, it is no loss. Firing them in the enemy's camp, a long way off, would prevent the enemy sleeping; and then if he does not sleep, then he gets ill and goes into hospital, and then needs other enemies to take care of him, and thus the enemy's numbers are reduced. When an enemy comes up and breaks the wall of the city, the Chinese soldiers ought not to stay and fight the enemy; but to go out and attack the trains of baggage in the rear, and worry him on the roads he came by. By keeping the Chinese troops lightly loaded with baggage, with no guns, they can move two to every one li the enemy marches. To-day the Chinese will be before him; to-morrow they will be behind him; the next day they will be on his left hand; and so on till the enemy gets tired and cross with such long walks, and his soldiers quarrel with their officers and get sick.

"The Chinese should make telegraphs in the country, as a rule, to keep the country quiet, and free from false rumours; but with the Chinese soldiers in the field, they should use sun-signals, by the means of the heliograph. These are very easy, and can do no harm. For this purpose a small school should be established in each centre. Chinese ought not to try torpedoes, which are very difficult to manage. The most simple torpedoes are the best and the cheapest, and their utility is in having many of them. China can risk sowing them thickly; for if one of them does go astray and sink a Chinese junk, the people of the junk ought to be glad to die for their country. If torpedoes are only used at certain places, then the enemy knows what he has to look out for when near these places; but when every place may have torpedoes, he can never feel safe; he is always anxious; he cannot sleep; he gets ill and dies. The fact of an enemy living in constant dread of being blown up is much more advantageous to China than if she blew up one of her enemies, for anxiety makes people ill and cross. Therefore China ought to have cheap simple torpedoes, which cannot get out of order, which are fired by a fuse, *not* by electricity, and plenty of them. She ought not to buy expensive complicated torpedoes.

"China should buy no more big guns to defend her sea-coast. They cost money. They are a great deal of trouble to keep in order, and the enemy's ships have too thick sides for any gun China can buy to penetrate them. China ought to defend her sea-coast by very heavy mortars. They cost very little; they are easy to use; they only want a thick parapet in front; and they are fired from a place the enemy cannot see, whereas the enemy can see the holes from which guns are fired. The enemy cannot get safe from a mortar-shot; it falls on the deck, and there it breaks everything. China can get 500 mortars for the same money she gets an 18-ton gun for. If China loses them, the loss is little. No enemy could get into a port which is defended by 15,000 large mortars and plenty of torpedoes, which must be very simple. Steam-launches, with torpedoes on a pole, furnish the best form of moveable torpedo. For the Chinese fleet, small quick vessels, with very light draught of water, and not any great weight of armour, are best. If China buys big vessels, they cost a great deal, and all her eggs are in one basket—namely, she loses all her money at once. For the money of one large vessel China could get twelve small vessels. China's strength is in the creeks, not in the open seas.

"Nothing recommended in this paper needs any change in Chinese customs. The army is the same, and China needs no Europeans or foreigners to help her to carry out this programme. If China cannot carry out what is here recommended, then no one else can do so. Besides, the programme is a cheap one.

"With respect to the fleet, it is impossible to consider that in the employment of foreigners China can ever be sure of them, in case of war with the country they belong to; while on the other hand, if China asks a foreign Power to lend her officers, then that foreign Power who lends them will interfere with her. The question is: (1) Is it better for China to get officers here and there, and run the risk of these officers not being trustworthy? or (2). Is it better for China to think what nation there is who would be likely to be good friends with China in good weather and in bad weather; and then for China to ask that nation to lend China the officers she wants for her fleet? I think No. 2 is the best and safest for China.

"Remember, with this programme, China wants no big officer from foreign Powers; I say big officer, because I am a big officer in China. If I stayed in China it would be bad for China, because it would vex the American, French, and German Governments, who would want to send their officers. Besides, I am not wanted. China can do what I recommend herself. If she cannot, I could do no good." *

Though Li Hungchang sympathised cordially with Gordon in his desire for peace, Prince Ch'un and his friends were by no means willing to yield at once, and Li was ordered to make every preparation for covering the capital against the attack of an invading force. Meanwhile every effort was being made by Li and his followers to obtain a reversal of the sentence of death which had been passed on Chung How. This action, coupled as

* *The Story of Chinese Gordon.* By A. E. HAKE; vol. i. pp. 379 385.

it was with strong recommendations to come to terms
with Russia, gave the Censors an opportunity, which
they eagerly took advantage of, to denounce the Viceroy
as a traitor to his country. They asked, and with some
appearance of reason, how it was that after Li had year
after year spent huge sums of money on ships and
armaments, the country should still be unprepared for
war. They further charged him with keeping up a secret
correspondence with Chung How in prison, and they
called for the infliction of an exemplary punishment upon
him. But Li was strong enough to resist these attacks.
His peace policy was carried out with the able assistance
of the Marquis Tsêng at St. Petersburg, and Chung How
was ultimately given his freedom. On the subject of
cession of territory, the treaty concluded by the Marquis
Tsêng with the Russian Government was a decided
improvement on that proposed by Chung How. The
Tekkes Valley and the passes through the T'ien Shan
into Kashgaria, were to remain in Chinese hands, but
the indemnity, which had been fixed by Chung How
at 5,000,000 metal roubles, was increased by Tsêng
to 9,000,000.

WITH the disappearance of this burning question, Li returned to the duties of provincial administration, though the scare which had startled the country still further emphasized in his mind the necessity of strengthening the defences of the empire. Port Arthur had lately been fortified and garrisoned, and Li determined to make a personal inspection of the new fortress. Accompanied by a fleet of gunboats he crossed the China Sea, and was received in state by Admiral Ting, who was in command. In times of peace Chinese naval officers are able to show off their ships to the best advantage, and Li was gratified by the sight of the manœuvres of the ships of the northern fleet, by the booming of the guns of the fortress, and by the spectacle of the sea illuminated at night with the electric light. Pleased with his inspection he returned to Peking, and forwarded to the throne a strong recommendation for the promotion of the officers who had so ministered to his gratification.

The province of Chihli, being the metropolitan district, has so strong a light thrown upon it that seditious movements are rarely heard of. In the beginning of 1882, however, Li discovered a heterodox sect, who, he reported to the Throne, "have been in the habit of worshipping an imaginary being called Piao Kao Lao Tsu (The Phantasmal high and ancient Ancestor), and unsettling the public mind by other superstitious observances. The ringleaders of the sect, Hsing Lê-chi and Hsing Lê-wei, when examined, stated that their society was divided into four branches, named after the four cardinal points, and met together four times a year for purposes of worship. Nothing beyond this could be established against the sect, which apparently had but few followers in Chihli, and had not been the cause, as yet, of any public disturbance. The two ringleaders have been dealt with according to the law on the subject, that is, sent to Urumtsi as slaves for the soldiery; and the remaining members of the association in custody have been sentenced to penalties less severe." *

These measures were presumably sufficient to crush the evil, even if, at any time, the society had possessed elements of danger in its constitution, and Li had now to turn to face another attack made upon him by the censors. It was well known that he had opened the Kai Ping coal mines near Tientsin, and that, with the aid of a tramway, this venture was returning a large revenue on the money laid out. Any stick, however, is good enough to beat a dog with, and the insensate censors brought the ridiculous charge against the Viceroy that by digging into the bowels of the earth he had so disturbed the pulse of the territorial dragon, and outraged the Fêngshui of the

* _Translation of the Peking Gazette_, Jan. 10th, 1882.

district, that the remains of the late Empress were unable to lie peacefully in the grave. Ridiculous as such a charge appears to Europeans, it has to the Chinese a distinct bearing and importance, so much so, that the censors' memorial on the subject was published at full length in the *Peking Gazette.* What means, if any, Li took to defeat this attack we have no means of knowing, but like those which had preceded it, it failed for an instant to shake the power of the great Viceroy, who well knew that he could confidently count on the firm and loyal support of the Empresses Regent and Prince Kung, to protect him from his enemies. Both as regards the internal and foreign policies of China, Li had long made up his mind, and, undeterred by the malice of his opponents, he pursued the system of developing the resources of the Empire, and of maintaining amicable relations with foreign countries, with undeviating firmness.

At the time, when the recent negotiations with Russia had been in a critical state, hints had been dropped at St. Petersburg that the Tzar's Government might possibly look for some compensation for restoring the province of Kudlja, in the acquisition of Port Lazaref, on the coast of Korea. It was well-known that Russia not unnaturally desired the possession of a port on the Pacific which was navigable all the year round, and the danger implied by the feelers thus put out made a profound impression on Li. He saw at once that the only sure way of protecting Korea against Russian invasion was to throw it open to foreign commerce, and thus to make it the interest of the majority of the Powers to protect it against the encroachments of any one of their number. He, therefore, memorialised the Throne, strongly urging that the Korean King should be advised to negotiate treaties with such Powers as desired to open relations with him; and in pursuance of this policy, treaties were arranged through Li's instrumentality, with the United States, Great Britain, and Germany.

Meanwhile, Li's active interference in affairs was temporarily put a stop to by a domestic bereavement. Early in 1882, his mother, who was an old lady of eighty-three, became seriously ill, and Li, who had had an opportunity of witnessing the success of the medical skill of Miss Howard, a medical missionary, in the treatment of his wife during a recent illness, invited that lady to attend his mother, who was lying ill at her son's residence at Wooch'ang. Being anxious himself also to visit his mother in her affliction, he presented the following curious memorial to the Throne, applying for leave of absence :—

"Memorial from Li Hungchang, stating that he has just received letters from home telling him that his mother is no better. He prays, therefore, that he may be granted leave of absence to go at once to visit her. He states that his mother, whose maiden name was Li [the same character as the Grand Secretary's] has been residing for some ten years in the official residence of his brother, Han-chang, the Governor-General of Hu-kuang. She is eighty-three years of age, and her constitution has hitherto been robust. But last winter she suffered from dysentery, and although the physicians succeeded in stopping the worst symptoms, she still continued feverish at night. At the beginning of spring she was a little better. Memorialist had earlier sent his son, Ching-fang, to Hu-pei to wait on his mother with food and medicine in his stead, but a letter which he has just received informs him that she is

affected with a continual cough, and cannot take food and
drink in any quantity. She is old and is breaking up : and
the thought of her absent son continually recurs to her,
and makes her illness more dangerous. When memorialist
heard this his heart burned with anxiety, and his sleep and
his food were worthless to him. And since the day in the
spring of 1870, when he left with his forces for Shèn-hsi,
and bade her farewell thirteen years ago, he has never
seen his mother's face. A man has a long life-time, it is
said, to spend in his country's service, and but a short
term of years in which he can serve his parents ; and now
that the illness from which his mother has long been
suffering, still continues unabated, memorialist all night
long tosses about in his trouble, and not for a single
moment is his mind at rest. It is, therefore, his bounden
duty to earnestly pray their Majesties for an unusual
extension of their gracious kindness, and to beg that they
will grant him a month's leave of absence. This will
enable him, he hopes, travelling along the coast and up the
river by steamer, so as to make a rapid journey to Wooch'ang, to visit his mother and to be a witness of her
recovery, and to satisfy, in some slight degree, the feeling
of affection which, as the jay for its parent bird, he enter-
tains for her. What bounds would be then set to his
gratitude for such signal kindness on the part of their
Majesties? If this should, indeed, be extended to him,
and his mother should by the favour of the Empress and
the Emperor see the son who has long been a wanderer,
return and wait on her, she perchance might be restored
to health. He would then go back with all speed to
Chihli, to perform the duties of his post. These, including
as they do the Superintendency of Trade for the northern
ports, the Directorship of the Coast Defence, and the
conduct of International Affairs, besides the government
of the province of Chihli, are of the gravest importance.
It is his duty then to pray that an official of standing
may be despatched to Tientsin to act provisionally in his
stead, and so prevent delay or miscarriage. The reason
for his application for leave, the wish, namely, to visit his
mother, he has carefully set forth on the present petition

to the Throne, which he is sending by courier post for
their Majesties' perusal and approval. He presents this
memorial with inexpressible fear and distress of mind." *

To this touching appeal the Empresses could not turn
a deaf ear, and, in reply, their Majesties granted to the
suppliant one month's leave of absence, and at the same
time graciously enclosed eight ounces of ginseng (*aralia
quinquefolia*, a medicine which is believed by the Chinese
to possess great regenerative powers) for the recovery of
his mother. Unhappily, the old lady passed away before
there was time either for Li to reach Wooch'ang, or for the
medicine to arrive, and as a matter of fact the news was
made known at Tientsin before the Viceroy had completed the arrangements for his departure. By the ritual
law of China a son is bound to mourn twenty-seven
months for a parent, and in the case of officials the same
oppressive code makes it incumbent on them to retire
from their posts for that period. On receiving the
announcement of his mother's death, therefore, Li at
once presented a memorial to the Throne, asking permission to be allowed to retire into private life for the
recognised time of mourning, and to resign his duties
as Grand Secretary and Viceroy of Chihli for the same
period.

Li, however, was too indispensable to the State to be
allowed to absent himself from the political world for
so long a time as two years and a quarter, and the
Regents therefore declined his request. In a decree,
which was published in the *Peking Gazette*, their Majesties
explained their refusal, and justified the departure from

* *Translation of the Peking Gazette*, May 16th, 1882.

established custom, which it implied, in the following terms :—

"Considering that Li Hungchang has long held the Viceroyalty of Chihli, and has acquitted himself carefully and successfully in the conduct of the numerous and important questions that have from time to time come before him, thereby obtaining our fullest confidence ; considering, moreover, that the different military divisions now garrisoning Chihli are all troops originally trained by him, and owe their efficiency to long service under him, and that the establishment and training of a naval contingent for the protection of the northern waters is an experiment of quite a novel character, the supervision of which cannot be well transferred to inexperienced hands ; and, lastly, considering the Viceroy's intimate acquaintance with the details of the foreign trade he has so long superintended, we have, after careful reflection, come to the conclusion that a modification of existing usage is here necessary. We, therefore, direct Li Hungchang, on the expiry of 100 days of mourning, to return with all despatch to his post and, retaining his present rank as Grand Secretary, to administer the province of Chihli as Acting Viceroy. The questions of the hour are attended with much difficulty, and the Viceroy should struggle to suppress his private sorrow, looking upon the affairs of State as of the first importance, and striving to make some return to us for our kindness to him. This will be the conduct that will inspire his mother's mind with the comforting conviction that her son, following the precepts early instilled into him, is devoting himself to the service of his country, and fervent is our hope (that this view of the matter will commend itself to the Viceroy)." *

Against these commands Li protested with all the eloquence of which he was capable, in the following memorial :—

* *Translation of the Peking Gazette,* April 26, 1882.

"A Memorial from Li Hungchang. On April 27th the Grand Council had the honour to receive the Imperial Decree, directing Memorialist to shorten the term of mourning. For this mark of kindness, and for the sympathy shewn by their Majesties in thus deigning to look into the secrets of his heart, he is deeply grateful. That he, with mean abilities, is not cast aside, but rather receives fresh honours, is cause for astonished gratitude and tears in all beholders ; much more, then, in him who is concerned, who cannot fail to be stimulated to fresh exertions. But Memorialist feels that he must submit the full expression of his feelings to their Majesties. It is twelve years since, in the dearth of officials, he was appointed to Chihli ; his shortcomings have been many, and his merits few ; he has repeatedly received marks of extraordinary consideration in being preserved intact in his dignities, and in not receiving censure and punishment. Then must he needs use his poor abilities to the utmost and maintain a resolute and grateful heart, not halting in the face of difficulties. But since he heard of his mother's severe illness, his brain has been dull and his eyes heavy. Leave of absence was granted him, but before he could start on his long journey, he received the letter telling of her death. Remorse will consequently haunt him all his life, and there is a wound in his heart that prevents him, privately, from enjoying a moment's respite from pain, and publicly from being of any service to the State. His conflicting duties as a Statesman and a dutiful son leave him perplexed and undecided. To those cases in this dynasty, where natural feeling has been put aside, much censure has attached. In 1851, while Tsêng Kwo-fan was driving the rebels out of Kiangsi, he was thrown into mourning by the death of his mother. The campaign was most important, and, as the law provides that a soldier in the field may not quit his post, it was held advisable that he should gird himself with black and remain with his troops ; but he repeatedly memorialised the Throne appealing against these orders, and persistently prayed to be allowed to keep the full term of mourning. Of late years, Li Hung-tsao, having lost his mother, prayed that he might observe the full period, and the Imperial assent was vouchsafed to his prayer. Even if Memorialist, separated, beyond hope of meeting, from his mother, the living from the dead, were to spend three years in lamentations at her tomb, it would not avail to relieve his soul from the poignant and inexpressible regret he feels for his lack of filial duty. But if, while stunned with grief, he is forced to rise in his mourning garb and attend to business, not only will violence be done to the grand principle of filial duty on which the Government is based, but comment, also, will be provoked on the shortcomings of the disciple of Confucius. Besides, though Memorialist holds high rank in the Grand Secretariat and an important post in the provinces, still, while his heart is torn with grief and his head is aching, how can he, with the evil omen of guilt attaching to him, lightly venture to retain those offices? Though trusted to the fullest extent by his Sovereign, a sense of shame would continue to harass him. He therefore prays their Majesties in pitying recognition of the reality of their foolish servant's grief, to recall their commands, and graciously permit him to vacate his posts and observe the full term of mourning; that the autumn frosts and spring dews may, in the course of time, witness some alleviation of his bitter regrets. But though the earth be his pillow, and his bed be of rushes, he is still beneath the canopy of heaven. He is but sixty years of age, and his stay in the thatched hut has a limit. Many are the days left in which to shew his gratitude to the State. Thus, little by little, now with loud weeping and now with silent sobs, has their Majesties' servant told them his piteous tale; and the anxiety with which he awaits their commands is beyond his power to express."

This appeal was confessedly urgent, but the political horizon was not sufficiently clear to justify the Regents in granting the Viceroy's request, and even during the hundred days allowed him for the gratification of his

grief, he was obliged, "though harassed by public and
private anxiety," to attend to his official duties.   In
accordance with Chinese custom, the funeral of the old
lady was postponed for several months that a day of
fortunate omen might be chosen for the ceremony.   As
the time approached, Li again memoralized the Throne,
asking for leave "to return home to bury his mother."
The observance of this duty is so sacred and recognised
a part of Chinese ritual life that it was impossible to
refuse the request, and two months' leave of absence was
granted to him.   With every outward manifestation of
pomp and woe, the old lady was carried to her grave, by
the side of which stood her two Vice-regal sons, Li
Hanchang and Li Hungchang, with their two brothers,
while twenty grandsons and eight great-grandsons joined
in the lamentations over her remains.   While this rite
was going on at the entombment, a striking ceremony
was being performed elsewhere.   With much state and
circumstance the memorial tablet of the deceased was
placed among the ancestral memorials of the Li family,
in the presence of three hundred Mandarins, who one
and all kotowed before the tablet in token of their respect
for the mother of the great Viceroys.   At the conclusion
of the funeral ceremony, Li returned to his post at
Tientsin, and took the opportunity of inspecting, by the
way, the various arsenals and forts which had owed their
existence to his initiative and fostering care.

On the third of September, 1883, Li took over the
seals of office as acting Viceroy of Chihli.   He still
desired or professed to desire to be relieved of duties
connected with that post, and of those pertaining to the

Grand Secretariat, and in a succession of memorials, he pleaded for permission to retire. But he was far too important a man to be allowed the luxury of seclusion, and in an equal number of decrees he was peremptorily forbidden to think of any such proceeding. To a man so fond of power as Li Hungchang, it is difficult to suppose that private life could possibly offer to him the attractions possessed by office, but if persistence is evidence of sincerity, it must be admitted that, strange as it may appear, on this occasion he was really in earnest, and it is equally obvious that the Regents expressed their full conviction, when they repeatedly told him that his prayer could not be granted. At last this Imperial and Vice-regal duel came to an end, and in September, 1884, a decree appeared reinstating Li in the offices of Viceroy, Superintendent of Foreign Trade, and Grand Secretary.

In the mean time, however, Li had not been idle, and had testified his interest in domestic and foreign politics, by the unceasingly active part which he took in them from behind the veil of mourning. Among the charitable institutions which owed their existence to his energy, was a most useful one which had been established at the time when the famine of 1878 was devastating the province of Chihli. This institution had been designed for the reception and maintenance of waifs and strays, and in the first instance had been confined only to the temporary accommodation of children left destitute by the famine. The continuance of the charitable work had been, however, found so necessary, that a permanent society had been established, for the endowment of which an appeal was made to the gentry of the neighbourhood. Subscriptions

were generously provided, and the committee soon found
themselves in a position to erect a building containing
two hundred and eight rooms, on a carefully selected site
outside the West gate of the city.

" The institution," wrote the Viceroy in his report on
the subject, at this time, to the Throne, " is divided into
six wards.   The first is devoted to the reception of
children of the male sex.   These are, immediately on
admittance, washed, divested of their rags, and medically
attended to.   They are then passed on to one of the
other wards.   No. 2 ward is a school where competent
teachers are engaged to instruct such of the children
as give evidence of an aptitude for study.   Those who
do not exhibit signs of such intelligence are relegated
to ward No. 3, where they are employed in agricultural
labour on the land adjoining the institution.   Those
whom a weak *physique* renders unfit for this labour,
and who have no taste for study, are taught various
handicrafts in ward No. 4.   No. 5 ward is reserved
for the relief of destitute female children, for whom
husbands are subsequently provided, and young widows
who do not intend to contract a second marriage.   The
sixth ward is devoted to the reception and cure of
confirmed opium smokers, who are attended by able
physicians armed with carefully selected drugs and pre-
scriptions, that their patients may be enabled to make
a fresh start in life, and that the State prohibitions of
this vice may not have been enunciated in vain.   Each
ward is placed under the superintendence of overseers
who possess special qualifications for the duties entailed
upon them, and the arrangement of the female department is particularly satisfactory.   This ward is kept
constantly under lock and key, food being passed in
to them by means of a revolving apparatus communicating with the outside.   The head of the department
is chosen from among aged widows of established
reputation, one of whose duties is to solicit, through
the proper authority, Imperial marks of approbation
for such of the inmates as have preserved their

chastity for a term of years sufficiently long to warrant the application on their behalf. The work achieved by the institution since its foundation has been most gratifying to its promoters. Over 2,000 opium smokers has been discharged with the craving thoroughly eradicated from their systems, a fact which cannot fail to have a highly beneficial effect on the public morals, and to afford encouragement to smokers as yet uncured. Memoralist then proceeds to state that the institution is still in working order, but its funds are low, and remembering the Imperial aid afforded in the reign of Tao Kwang to a similar establishment at Pao-ting Fu, which had been the means of relieving fifty young girls and widows—whereas the Kuang-jen T'ang has already admitted more than 750 of these, besides innumerable applicants of other descriptions—he ventures to beg of His Majesty a yearly gift of 300 piculs of rice towards the support of this charity.—Granted by Rescript." *

But towards the close of his enforced mourning, Li's attention was diverted from domestic and charitable interests by a political event, which has already had far-reaching consequences. As has already been mentioned, Li had for some time strongly urged the King of Korea to enter into relations with Foreign States for the protection of his kingdom, and the advice had been well received. There was, however, a powerful party in the country which had from the first objected to the Japanese Alliance, and which was still more opposed to the Treaties with the European Powers. The news, therefore, of Li's advice banded together these opponents to change, who determined to strike a blow for what they believed to be the liberty of their country, rather than submit to the state of things which they

* *Translation of the Peking Gazette,* May 19, 1882.

regarded as unendurable. A Japanese Legation had
been already established at Seoul, and it was on these
visitors that the malcontents first opened their attack.
On the 23rd July, 1882, the Japanese Minister, Mr.
Hanabusa, received a message from the Governor of
Seoul warning him that a dangerous riot had broken
out in the city, which the Governor feared was mainly
directed against him and his countrymen.

The results proved that the Governor was right, for after
some trifling rioting in the city, the mob marched directly
on the Japanese Legation. For a time the diplomatists
succeeded in keeping the rioters at bay, but a torch having
been successfully applied to the buildings in the neighbourhood of the Legation, their position became untenable.
With steady courage the staff, who numbered about forty
persons, sallied out against the mob, and fought their way
to the port of Chemulpo, where they fortunately found a
British gunboat, in which they embarked for Japan.

It was well known that the leader in this outbreak was
the ex-Regent, and father of the King, Li Shih-ying.
During the period of the young king's minority, this man
had persistently pursued an anti-foreign policy. It was
under his regime that the French and American expeditions which had visited Korea had been attacked, and it
was at his instigation that the French missionaries resident
in the country had been hunted to death. Though thus
personally hostile to foreigners, he had been unable to
convince the king, his son, of the wisdom of his views,
and so soon as the young sovereign came of age and
succeeded to power, an entirely opposite policy had been
pursued. It was said that the Queen had been an active

supporter of the King's views, to which an acquaintance with the peaceful doctrines of Christianity had inclined her. But, however that may be, the struggle which was now going on was practically a contest between the progressive and reactionary parties in the state. The outbreak represented a bid for power on the ex-Regent's part, and for a time it seemed probable that he would be successful. The young King was made a prisoner in his palace, and the Queen was said to have been murdered. Happily this last rumour proved to be unfounded. With the help of her friends she succeeded in gaining for herself a place of shelter, while, with rare devotion, one of the ladies of the Court remained to personate her royal mistress and met death in her stead.

Meanwhile the news of the outbreak was carried with all speed to Peking, and Li was ordered to take immediate steps to restore peace. As has already been pointed out, the Viceroy possesses that very useful instinct of attaching to himself men of ability and action. For some years he had had on his staff a Mandarin named Ma Chien-chung, whom, on many occasions, he had employed on missions requiring tact and discretion. It so happened that just at this time Ma had returned from India, whither he had been sent by his chief to enquire into matters connected with the opium trade. The crisis which had now arisen was precisely one in which Ma's ability and finesse would find congenial scope. Without a moment's hesitation, therefore, Li despatched him to Seoul with a fleet of iron-clads and a considerable force of soldiers. At the same time the Mikado sent Mr. Hanabusa with a large and well-equipped escort to Korea to uphold the rights and dignity of Japan. The presence of these opposing forces brought the two countries within measurable distance of war. Japan had not only made a treaty with Korea, but had claimed to exercise over the country an equal suzerainty with China, by right of previous conquests. Happily, owing to Ma's diplomacy and Hanabusa's moderation, all active hostility was avoided, and the Chinese were able to suppress entirely all outward manifestations of anti-foreign feeling. But Li well knew that so long as the ex-Regent was allowed his liberty there must always be danger of reactionary disturbances, and Ma took with him instructions to seize and carry off the turbulent ex-Regent if, in the exercise of his discretion, he should deem it wise so to do. Events plainly pointed in Ma's opinion to the wisdom of this course of action, and he proceeded to carry it out with alacrity. Throughout his negotiations he had been careful to maintain amicable relations with the ex-Regent, and at one of his interviews he, in a friendly way, invited him to dinner on board his ship. With unsuspecting confidence Li Shih-ying accepted the proffered hospitality, and was no sooner safely on board than he was told that he was to consider himself a prisoner, and that, as a measure of precaution, he was to be carried off to China. On the arrival of the State prisoner at Tientsin, Li reported to the Throne the measures which he had adopted, and in responce to his memorial the following Decree was issued :—

   "*A Decree.*—Korea is a dependency of China. Its princes have, for generations, been our feudatories, and have ever been known to be reverent and respectful. The Court regards them as its near kindred, and we sympathize in their joys and sorrows. Some time since Chang Shu-shêng reported to us that the Korean army had mutinied, and had suddenly, in the 6th moon, surrounded the palace of the Prince; that the Princess had come to an untimely end, and Ministers of State had been slain; that the Japanese Legation also had suffered from their violence. We forthwith ordered Chang Shu-shêng to send land and naval forces to put down the rebellion, and, as Li Hungchang's period of leave had expired, we summoned him to Tientsin to assist in the settlement of the affair. Shortly after, the General Wu Ch'ang-fa and Sing Fu-ch'ang, and the Intendant Ma Chien-chung, crossed to Korea at the head of an army, and making their way into the capital, seized on over 100 of the rebels. They exterminated the ringleaders, but pardoned their followers, and in the space of ten days, the trouble and disturbance were allayed, and general confidence restored. Inquiry into the common talk of the people showed that the cause of the outbreak was the soldiers' clamouring for pay, and that it was Li Shih-ying who was the arch-plotter in inciting them to mutiny. Wu Ch'ang-fa and his colleagues accordingly sent him under escort to Tientsin; and we sent down orders that he should be handed over to Li Hungchang and Chang Shu-shêng, who should ascertain the facts and report to us. Li Shih-ying, when the Prince was of tender years, held the supreme authority and oppressed the people. His misdeeds are plainly evident. Ever since the Prince assumed the government, his jealousy has daily increased. Last year there was a conspiracy to rebel on the part of his son, Li Tsai-hsien; and, when, on this occasion, the disaffected soldiery, first of all, proceeded to his house to make known their grievances, he did not with firm remonstrances dissuade them from insurrection; on the contrary, when the riot was over, he usurped the government. His power and supremacy were unlimited; but he took no steps to punish the rebels. When Li Hungchang and his colleague, in obedience to our command, examined him, he persisted in every conceivable prevarication and concealment, and would not confess the truth. His assembling a band of rebels, his being the prime-mover in this outbreak, assuredly render him liable to a hundred penalties, which he cannot evade. Considering the constant arrogance with which he has intimidated his sovereign, and his plot that endangered the state, he should be punished with all the rigour of the law. But we think ourselves of the ties of kindred that render Li Shih-ying an object of reverence to the Prince of Korea, and that, if heavy sentence be meted out to him, that Prince will be involved in a state of helpless misery. For these reasons, we, of our special favour, most leniently lighten his sentence. Let Li Shih-ying escape the punishment due to his crimes, and live in peace at Paoting Fu in Chihli, nor ever return to his country. Let the Governor-General of Chihli continue to bountifully afford him such support as his rank demands, and strictly keep watch over him, that thus a cause of trouble and calamity to Korea may be removed, and the breach of the laws of kindred towards the Prince of that kingdom be healed. Wu Ch'ang-fa's force is to remain for the present in Korea to preserve order, and Li Hungchang is to attend to the settlement of that kingdom." *

While Ma was providing for the removal and safe custody of this Korean firebrand, Japan was formulating the conditions which she was prepared to accept as compensation for the insult offered to her flag. She demanded that the Korean Government should pay the sum of 500,000 dollars as an indemnity for the cost of the expedition ; that a new treaty port should be opened to trade ; that a mission of apology should be sent to Japan ; and that the Minister should have the right to maintain an escort of troops at the Legation for the period of one year at least. These points were all conceded, but as a token of friendly feeling the Mikado's Government

* *Translation of the Peking Gazette,* Sep. 23, 1882.

volunteered to forego four-fifths of the indemnity in consideration of the poverty-stricken condition of the Korean people.

Li Hungchang was the more anxious to come to terms with Japan on this occasion, as it was becoming more and more obvious that while, in the main, the armaments of his countrymen were such as their ancestors had rejoiced in, the Japanese had been making strenuous efforts to provide their army with the newest weapons invented at Elswick and by Krupp. Already secret memorials had been presented to the Throne on this subject, among others by Chang P'eilun, a clever, ambitious, shifty man, who is now the son-in-law of Li Hungchang. This paper, which was presented to the Throne in 1882, and which has recently been published, reveals the apprehension with which well-informed Chinamen regarded the reforms which were being rapidly introduced into the Japanese army. While asserting that the military system of Japan was not well organised, and that the soldiers in the ranks were inferior to those marshalled under Li's banners, the writer was still of opinion that since Japan was venturing upon a display of power, and had not only taken possession of the Loo Choo Islands, but was even making attempts on Korea, it had become the duty of "our Empire to check in time the threatening peril from Japan, and to establish definitely the supremacy of China over its neighbour." It was impossible to deny, however, that an attack upon Japan would be a hazardous undertaking, and Chang, therefore, urged on his Imperial master the necessity of adding strength and efficiency to the navy and army of China.

This memorial was forwarded to Li for his opinion, and in reply the Viceroy presented to the Throne the following carefully written paper :—

"I have had the honour of receiving the Imperial Edict of the 16th of the seventh month, forwarded by the Board of Military Affairs and enclosing a memorial of Chang-P'ei-lun, on which I am ordered by your Majesty to express my opinion as to our future relations with Japan.

"Some time ago, when I was ordered by your Majesty to offer my opinion on the questions raised by the memorial of Ten-sen-sue, the member of the Board of Government Inspectors, I felt compelled to maintain views which were contrary to his, but under the present circumstances I cannot but express my entire concurrence with the views of Chang-P'ei-lun—namely, that it is necessary for us to make preparations for a war with Japan, and that, consequently, we must develop our naval armaments in order to be able to carry out this object.

"For some years past we have already been actively engaged on these preparations, and our best efforts have been directed towards the reorganization of our navy and army. Enormous sums of money have been spent in order to enable us to display our power and to assert our superiority over our neighbour, whenever the moment favourable for this attempt shall have arrived.

"The convention lately concluded between Korea and Japan is, however, only a consequence of the attack on the Japanese Legation in Korea, committed by Korean conspirators, and followed by a massacre of Japanese residents in Sôul; it is evident that on this question we have no right to interfere. In the treaty between Korea and Japan the latter recognizes the former as an independent State, without any regard to us, but respecting this we must remember that China never recognized the independence of Korea—a course in which other Powers have agreed with us, and has led them to assume an attitude opposed to that of Japan.

"Therefore our best case for bringing about a rupture with Japan and coming to extremities is not Korea, but the question of the Loo-Choo Islands, because we have an indisputable right over them, and every foreign Power would be obliged to admit the justice of our claim, if we chose to demand the restoration of our rights.

"The actual situation of Japan is such that it is labouring under financial difficulties and suffering under the burdens of an oppressive national debt. The continual struggles between the two political parties, Satsuma and Choshiu, affect its power, and the weakness of its navy and army is admitted. Japan has, however, ever since the restoration, tried its best to establish a good understanding with foreign nations, and the Japanese hope to preserve their independence by the aid of foreign influence. Hence the Government has despatched in the course of this year the Minister of State Ito to Europe, to inquire into the systems of European civil administration. Also the Imperial Prince Arisugawa has been sent to Russia to pay a visit to the Imperial Court, whilst diplomatic envoys were also appointed to Italy in rapid succession. These obsequious efforts of Japan in promoting international intercourse have produced a favourable impression abroad; the Japanese envoys have been welcomed and the foreign Powers seem not indisposed to render assistance to Japan, to a certain extent. It must, therefore, be borne in mind that there is a probability that in case of a conflict between China and Japan foreign Powers might side with Japan against us.

"But let us remember the two great principles, the motive force of which has a paramount influence—the moral power of reason, which distinguishes between right and wrong, and the material power of strength, which becomes might when opposed to weakness. Morally we are undoubtedly in our right on the question of the Loo-Choo Islands, and materially China is a large and strong empire, superior to Japan. If we only organize our resources, develop our army and navy, we shall gain the respect of even the more powerful of the foreign nations, who will rank us with the Great Powers, and then Japan will, of course, not venture to carry out any hostile designs against us (by means of a foreign alliance).

"But if Japan should, perchance, discover prematurely what our plans in preparing for a campaign against her are, the direct consequences will be that the Japanese Government and people would at once reunite and pull together; that they would enter into a close alliance with foreign Powers, and accumulate money by augmenting the national debt; that their naval power would be increased by the building and purchasing of ships; and that thus we should be placed in a disadvantageous position, pregnant with danger.

"In one of the ancient maxims it is said, 'Nothing is so dangerous as to expose one's scheme before it is ripe.' On this account I have in my former memorial recommended to your Majesty that we should be extremely cautious and take care to conceal our object, whilst neglecting nothing to raise our strength in the meantime.

"In times of great peril to the country the man who directs the affairs of State is obliged to act without hesitation, according to what he may consider at the moment the best for the nation. His success or failure depends, however, entirely on whether the time was favourable at the moment of his action. If the time is not favourable the man, however experienced or distinguished, must fail in carrying out his plans. This may be proved historically. During the era of the Sung Dynasty the the troops of Tsu-koh-liang were unsuccessful in Kohanchion. Hangchi as well as Fan-chiou were both experienced and learned Ministers; still, they failed in the subjugation of the small country of Shi-sha, which rebelled in the western part of the Chinese Empire. Again, in the reign of the Emperor Kao-tsung (the fourth Emperor of the present dynasty), when the Emperor extended the dominion of the empire to Central Asia and the glory of the Chinese nation had reached its climax, the two excellent generals—Tu-hen (Fu Hêng) and Yo-chiou-chi (Yo Chungchi)—failed to conquer Chin-Ch'uan, though only a small tribe in the province of

Szech'uen; whilst Aqui (Ah Kwei) and A-Ho-Koen (Ah Lekun), the ablest Ministers of the Emperor, were unsuccessful in the war against Burmah. In all these instances the failure must be attributed to the fact of the time not being propitious, besides the disadvantages arising from unfavourable geographical conditions.

"Japan has now for years earnestly studied Western systems, and, though her success is so far only an outward one, still, her fleet must be admitted to be equal to ours. Therefore, I should consider it hazardous to send our fleet to Japan to fight in the enemy's own waters. My humble opinion is, let us not lose sight of our plan of invading Japan, but let us not commit the mistake of doing this in a hurried manner. First of all, our navy must be thoroughly organised before we can think of an invasion.

"Your Majesty has graciously ordered me to undertake the responsibility of preparing the plan for the invasion of Japan. Allow me, therefore, to state that I consider this question one of the utmost importance to the Empire, and I fear that unless all the Ministers of the Cabinet and the Viceroys of all the provinces agree together, and assiduously work for years to come, any such an attempt would be a failure.

"When, during the Tai-ping Rebellion, our Government ordered the Viceroys to put down the rebels, each in his respective province, and each employing the resources of his own jurisdiction only, without the assistance of the others, this order turned out to be ineffective. The Viceroys were hampered in their efforts, and the rebellion spread from place to place. But when our Government changed this plan of dividing the power, and ordered the Viceroys to co-operate and join their forces, matters soon improved. Additional facilities were provided for massing the troops, large supplies could be stored, and the responsibility of punishing subordinate officials was divided; thus great effects were realised and the rebellion completely suppressed.

"Living now in a period of great tranquility, the ancient laws and regulations are strictly observed, consequently the Civil Service is only open to those men who have obtained the distinctions of a literary examination. Great difficulties exist, therefore, in obtaining other useful persons for the government service, for we are limited to the narrow compass of those qualified by passing the examinations ; also, in respect to the supplies necessary for the army, we find ourselves placed in the dilemma of having to come to a previous agreement with the several Viceroys and departments, arrangements which require a great deal of time and labour.

" It is absolutely necessary that if we should desire to secure the services of useful persons, we must introduce another system for their admission into the public service. In the interest, also, of a harmonious and united working of the Viceroys and Governors of the provinces, it will be necessary to adopt a method by which the quasi independent position, which they enjoy in their relations to each other, should be reformed and joint action secured.

" If your Cabinet Ministers and Viceroys will agree together, and your Majesty will rule over them all, in conformity with your own august decisions, then the invasion of Japan can be thought of, but it is decidedly better not to place the responsibility of this enterprise on my shoulders alone.

"Chang P'eilun, in his memorial, says that the want of success of our policy was mainly caused by the fact that the decisions of our Cabinet were rather unsettled, and the responsibility of the Ministers not clearly defined. I recognise this as being perfectly true, and constituting an indisputable fact.

" To give an instance. The necessity of creating a strong navy, and therefore the decision to build ships of war, was fully agreed upon by all the Ministers and Viceroys, and as funds were absolutely necessary, in order to purchase armaments, as well as for the maintenance of the army, the financial department of our Government fixed upon an annual appropriation of four million taels for the expenditure of the navy and for the purposes of coast defence. This amount was to be provided from the revenue of the Inland Custom duties. Unfortunately the estimate of the income was not founded on any solid basis, and it was afterwards found that the expenses of collecting the revenue in every province exceeded the amount collected. Besides, the amounts collected in the provinces of Fukien and Kwangtung was spent there, and nothing was paid by them into the Imperial Treasury. In consequence, my department received not the amount of four millions, which had been decided upon, but only one fourth of that sum. This deficiency in the income had for its natural consequence that it prevented the growth of our navy and the organisation of our coast defences.

"I beg humbly to express the hope that your Majesty will graciously order the Department of the Imperial Treasury and the Foreign Department of the Imperial Government to make out an accurate estimate of the contributions to be supplied by every province in support of the coast defence, whilst an additional amount should be granted for the defence of Formosa. Any deficiency should be made good by the Imperial Treasury, so that altogether a yearly amount of four million taels be brought together for naval expenditure, and this should be punctually paid into my department. Under these conditions I should be able to organise in five years a strong navy, and sufficiently organise our coast defence.

"In my humble opinion, Formosa and the Province of Shantung are the most important points of the Chinese Empire which should be secured against a Japanese attack, whilst the ablest generals should be selected to command these defences.

"Respecting the particulars of the invasion of Japan, I have already expressed my views in my former memorial; it is needless to refer to this here again.

"I resume my humble opinion as follows: —'That it is above all necessary to strengthen our country's defences, to organise a powerful navy, and the aggressive steps against Japan should not be undertaken in too great a hurry.'" *

* *The Times*, January 19, 1895.

CHAPTER XI.

THE foregoing paper explains the peaceable attitude of China during the negotiations with Japan with regard to Korea. Li Hungchang was far-sighted enough to recognise that the Chinese army was quite incapable of meeting either the troops of Japan or of any European power on equal terms. The central motive of his foreign policy was, therefore, to preserve peace, and, if circumstances should become too strong for him, and war supervene, to come to terms with the enemy while he should be in the way with him.

This conciliatory attitude was also conspicuous in his dealings with the French in the matter of Tongking. It will be remembered that so far back as 1873 the French had been making advances against that province, and that an agreement, which had been proposed in the interests of peace, and by which China bound herself to hand over to France that portion of the country which was south of the Songkoi River, had been finally rejected both at Paris and at Peking. Matters were in this position in 1884, when the Chinese became so seriously alarmed at the aggressive spirit displayed by France, that the Marquis Tsêng, the Chinese Minister at the Quai D'Orsay, was directed to warn the French Government that the Imperial Cabinet would regard an attack on the towns of Sontay and Bacninh as a declaration of war. At that time the French were by no means inclined to hold their hands, and disregarding the Marquis's communication, they attacked and occupied the two cities in question. The position now assumed the anomalous aspect of two Powers carrying on warlike operations in time of peace, for war was never declared. Li Hungchang had, from the first, striven to prevent the outbreak of hostilities, and circumstances subsequently arose, which enabled him to make an effort to carry out this pacific policy.

It chanced that at this juncture Mr. Detring, whose name has lately been associated with a futile attempt to open negotiations with Japan, returned from leave in Europe, to take up an official post at Canton. At Hong Kong he met Admiral Lespès and Captain Fournier, with whom he steamed up the river to the provincial capital. The sight of the very undefended condition of that city, and the very inefficient condition of the provincial forces, suggested to him the idea of opening negotiations for peace. He found the Viceroy of Canton anxious to follow his advice, but powerless to enter into negotiations; and after some discussion, therefore, he determined to put Captain Fournier in communication with Li on the matter.

On arriving at Tientsin, Captain Fournier found Li well disposed to listen to his propositions. The Viceroy had already pointed out to the Throne the gross blunders that had been committed during the campaign in Tongking, and threw the principal blame for the series of disasters, which had overtaken the Chinese arms, on the Governor of Kwangsi, who was, he declared, ignorant of the first rudiments of the art of war. It was to the hands of such men as this, he felt, that the fortunes of the empire were entrusted, and he repeatedly warned the Tsungli Yamên that the only hope left for the country was to make peace on almost any terms. He was prepared, therefore, at once to discuss matters with Captain Fournier so soon as he should receive plenipotentiary powers from Peking. At first his memorials to the Throne on the subject were coldly received, and at a council at which Prince Ch'un, the father of the Emperor, and twenty-seven other high officials took part, it was unanimously decided to reject Li's prayer. Fortunately, wiser counsels ultimately prevailed, and the Viceroy was relieved by receiving instructions to agree to the best terms which he could get from the French. Captain Fournier had in the meantime received by telegram plenipotentiary powers. With much secrecy the two representatives met in conclave, and finally on the 11th May, 1884, it was announced to the world that a convention had been drawn up and signed by the two plenipotentiaries.

"The Government of the French Republic and His Majesty the Emperor of China," so ran this document, "wishing by means of a preliminary Convention, the stipulations of which will constitute the basis of a definite Treaty, to put an end to the crisis which, at the present moment, has such a prejudicial effect on public order and commercial operations generally, wishing also to restore without delay, and to ensure for ever that good neighbourly intercourse and friendship which should exist between the two nations, have named as their respective Plenipotentaries—first, His Majesty the Emperor of China, His Excellency Li Hungchang, grand presumptive guardian of His Majesty the Emperor's son, First Secretary of State, Viceroy of Pechili, Hereditary Noble of the First Class of the Third Rank ; secondly, the Government of the French Republic, M. Ernest François Fournier, Captain in the Navy, Commander of the *Volta*, Officer of the Legion of Honour, who, after exchanging their credentials, which were found in due form, agreed to the following articles :—

" By the first Article France undertakes to respect and, in case of need, to protect the southern frontier of China, which separates that country from Tong-King. On her side China, reassured concerning the integrity and security of her southern frontier, undertakes immediately to withdraw to within the Chinese frontier the Chinese troops garrisoned in Tong-King. She, moreover, engages herself to respect in the present and future the Treaties concluded, or to be concluded, between France and the Court of Annam.

" Article 3 stipulates that, in recognition of the conciliatory attitude of China, and as a mark of appreciation of His Excellency Li's patriotic wisdom in the negotiation of this Convention, France consents to refrain from demanding an indemnity of China. In return for this, China engages to admit along the whole extent of her frontier bordering on Tong-King the liberty of commercial exchanges between Annam and France on the one hand and China (Yunnan, Kwangsi, and Kwangtung) on the other. With that object in view, a Treaty of commerce and tariffs shall be concluded in the most conciliatory spirit on the part of the Chinese negotiators, and under as advantageous conditions as possible for French commerce. Lastly, immediately after the signature of the Convention, the two Governments will appoint their Plenipotentiaries, who will meet within three months to negotiate the definitive Treaty on the basis thus established."

The conclusion of this Convention was celebrated by a grand dinner, given by Li to Captain Fournier and all those who had taken part in the negotiations. But the happy forecasts which found utterance at this feast were not destined to gain fulfilment. The conditions which the Convention contained no sooner became known in Peking and Paris than violent opposition was offered to their ratification. In China the Censors took up their pens as one man, and forty-seven memorials were presented to the Throne demanding the impeachment of Li-Hungchang as a traitor to his country. So fierce was the storm that Li was half inclined to bow before it, and it is said that he even asked leave of the Empress to be allowed to retire into private life. If it is true that this request was put forward, it is certain that it was refused, and, at all events, we know that though mortified by the frustration of his immediate hopes for peace, Li took up his cross and returned to the ordinary duties of his Viceroyalty.

Unfortunately for the prospects of peace an incident occurred which gave encouragement to the war-party in Peking, and to the fire-eaters of the Boulevardes. It will be observed that in the Convention, as published in the *Journal Official*, China agreed to withdraw all her troops garrisoning Tongking, but it is noticeable that no mention is made as to the date by which the troops were to be withdrawn, though in a subsequent note this, according to Capt. Fournier, was distinctly stated. On receiving notice of the Convention, in Tongking, Colonel

Dugenne, who was commanding the French troops in the neighbourhood of Langson, marched on that town and demanded its immediate surrender. In reply the Chinese Commandant acknowledged his obligation to retire, but asked that time might be given him to make the necessary arrangements for the evacuation of the city. Colonel Dugenne, apparently considering that the Chinese General was attempting to evade the conditions of the Convention, sternly replied that he would give him one hour and not a minute beyond to march out of the town. As the Chinaman was unable to execute so hasty a retreat Colonel Dugenne opened an attack, and was driven back with considerable loss.

War now again became inevitable, and the incident was used by the Chinese to illustrate the treacherous nature of Frenchmen and the folly of Li in trusting to them. Captain Fournier averred that he had agreed with Li as to the dates on which the fortresses were to be given up ; while Li, on the other hand, asserted that when he protested against the dates named as impracticable, Captain Fournier ran his pen through the clauses in dispute. In support of his view Captain Fournier addressed the following letter to Monsieur Ferry :—

"I affirm, upon my honour, that I neither altered nor cancelled, either by erasures or in any other way, any of the dates and stipulations of the note of May 17th, handed to Li Hungchang. I affirm that Li Hungchang expressly told me that the evacuation of the Chinese garrisons would be effected by him within the time fixed in that note. I affirm that it was with his entire assent that I addressed to the President of the Council (Monsieur Ferry) and to General Millot the telegrams inserted in the yellow book. I may add that I gave all possible publicity to the agreement concluded

in this last interview. I reported it immediately to
Admiral Lespés, who had to see the Viceroy on the
very next day and converse with him on the same
subject. I handed in the telegram sent by me to
General Millot, in French, at the Chinese telegraph office
in Tientsin, where all the officials are the functionaries
of the Viceroy's Yamén. An hour afterwards Li Hungchang had this telegram in his hand, which he could
read, and which, like all political telegrams, was trans-
mitted to the Tsungli Yamén. Such a step taken by the
French negotiator ; the Viceroy's silence, after all the
opportunities thus given him of protesting against the
telegram which he had in his hands, and which so
distinctly committed him — a telegram which was then
published in the Chinese newspapers, and the stipulations
and dates of which were publicly read on May 20th
before the Chamber of Deputies, by the President of
the Council. Can they leave the slightest doubt as
to the perfect certainty on my part, that no misunderstanding could exist between the Viceroy and myself
on the questions treated in the note on May 17th?"

But a misunderstanding did without question exist,
and, by Li's direction, his two secretaries gave the
following public denial to Captain Fournier's statements. In a letter addressed to the *North China
Herald*, those gentlemen wrote :—

"SIR,—Being informed that Captain Fournier, in a
letter that has been made public, denies having made
the erasures in the Fournier Memorandum presented to
Li Chungt'ang on the 17th of May last, we beg to state
that we were present at the interview Captain Fournier
had with His Excellency on that day, and we positively
declare that we saw with our own eyes Captain Fournier
with his own hand make the said erasures and put his
initials thereto.

"We remain, yours obediently,

"MA KIENCHUNG.
"LO FANGLO."

The war was now renewed with vigour, and it was only after severe fighting that General Négrier was able to capture Langson on the 13th February, 1885, which, but for the precipitancy of Colonel Dugenne, would have been given up nearly a year before. Still no declaration of war was issued, and this anomalous condition of affairs was productive of some strange incidents. Admiral Courbet, after some ineffectual operations on the coast of Formosa, entered the harbour of Foo-chow as though peace had never been broken, and having steamed past the batteries which defended the entrance, opened fire on the Chinese fleet which were assembled behind them. The official charged with the defence of the coast at Foo-chow was Chang P'eilun, of whom mention has already been made. This officer had ample warning of the approach of the French fleet, but neglected to make any preparations whatever to ward off a possible attack, and even had the audacity, when his fleet was finally destroyed, to report that he had gained a complete victory, and had sunk two of the French ironclads. This imposition was too obvious when read by the light of subsequent events to be passed over, and Chang was exiled for his offence to a place beyond the Great Wall. His patron, however, was powerful enough to secure before long his recall, and he now basks in the sunshine of Imperial favour.

With varying fortunes the war was continued for another year, until in January, 1886, a treaty was concluded between Monsieur Cogordan, a special envoy from France, and Li Hungchang. In anticipation of an

easy diplomatic victory Monsieur Cogordan came to
China with the treaty, ready prepared for signature,
in his pocket. But Li would have none of it. He
was well aware that the French were weary of the very
barren contest they had been wagering, and, armed with
this knowledge, he finally concluded a treaty which was
practically the same as the Convention he had arranged
with Monsieur Fournier in 1884. The result of these
negotiations was eminently confirmatory of Li's prescience,
for after a further year's conflict, which had cost the
country 60,000,000 taels, and had conduced to the
destruction of the fleet at Foo-chow, China eventually
accepted the identical terms which the Viceroy had
obtained before the 60,000,000 taels had been spent
or the fleet sunk.

Meanwhile affairs had been again disturbed in Korea.
The ex-Regent, who, it will be remembered, had been
interned at Paoting Fu had, without due consideration,
been allowed to return to his native country. The un-
wisdom of this proceeding quickly became apparent. No
sooner had he reached Seoul than he at once began his
old occupation of intriguing against the King. Every
reform and improvement which was set on foot by
the Sovereign was opposed à l'outrance by his father,
and on the occasion of a dinner given to commemorate
the inauguration of a new postal system the storm
which had long been carefully brewed broke out. The
banquetting hall, in which the Royal guests were
assembled, was invaded by a band of rebels, who
attempted to take the King prisoner. For four days
the fight raged between the contending factions, and

the Japanese were, for the second time, compelled to fight their way to the sea. The instant the news of this outbreak reached Tōkiō the Japanese despatched a force to Chemulpo for the protection of their country-men. The arrival of this expedition was the signal for a Chinese army to advance on Seoul. Thus again the position of 1882 was repeated, and for a second time there seemed to be every prospect of an outbreak of war between the two suzerain Powers. Happily, the danger was averted, and Count Ito was finally sent to Tientsin, to negotiate a treaty with Li Hungchang, which should determine the positions of the two countries as regards Korea.

It has lately been remarked that this treaty has hitherto never been published. We therefore give it in *extenso*.

"Convention between China and Japan for the with-drawal of Chinese and Japanese troops from Korea.— Signed at Tientsin, April 18, 1885.

" Ito, Ambassador Extraordinary of the Great Empire of Japan, Minister of State and the Imperial Household, First Class of the Order of the Rising Sun, and Count of the Empire ;

" Li, Special Plenipotentiary of the Great Empire of China, Grand Guardian of the Heir Apparent, Senior Grand Secretary of State, Superintendent of the North Sea Trade, President of the Board of War, Viceroy of Chihli and Count Shiriu-ki of the first rank ;

" In obedience to the Decrees which each of them respectively is bound to obey, after conference held, have agreed upon a Convention with a view to preserving and promoting friendly relations (between the two great Empires), the Articles of which are set down in order as follow :—

" It is hereby agreed that China shall withdraw her troops now stationed in Corea, and that Japan shall

withdraw hers stationed therein for the protection of
her Legation. The specific term for effecting the same
shall be four months, commencing from the date of the
signing and sealing of this Convention, within which term
they shall respectively accomplish the withdrawal of the
whole number of each of their troops, in order to avoid
effectively any complications between the respective
countries : the Chinese troops shall embark from
Masan-Po and the Japanese from the port of Ninsen.

"The said respective Powers mutually agree to invite
the King of Corea to instruct and drill a sufficient armed
force, that she may herself assure her public security, and
to invite him to engage into his service an officer or
officers from amongst those of a third Power, who shall
be entrusted with the instruction of the said force. The
respective Powers also bind themselves, each to the other,
henceforth not to send any of their own officers to Corea
for the purpose of giving said instruction.

"In case of any disturbance of a grave nature
occurring in Corea, which necessitates the respective
countries or either of them to send troops to Corea,
it is hereby understood that they shall give, each to the
other, previous notice in writing of their intention so to
do, and that after the matter is settled, they shall withdraw their troops and not further station them there.

"Signed and sealed this 18th day of the 4th month,
of the 18th year of Meiji (Japanese Calendar) : the
4th day of the 3rd moon of the 11th year of Kocho
(Kwang-hsü, Chinese Calendar).

> (L.S.) "ITO, *Ambassador Extraordinary of the Great
> Empire of Japan, &c.*
> (L.S.) "LI, *Special Plenipotentiary of the Great
> Empire of China, &c.*"*

Mid all these wars and rumours of wars Li had many
national causes of disquiet; not the least of which was
his difficulty in dealing with the China Merchants' Steam
Navigation Company. That affair had never really

prospered in a financial sense. Though nominally a company, it was to all intents and purposes an official undertaking. The shareholders were never consulted as to the management, and complained bitterly of the way in which their profits disappeared. In 1885 Li presented a Memorial to the Throne which disclosed facts which fully justified these lamentations. Two Taot'ais, whose particular offices in connection with the Company it is somewhat difficult to determine, except that they were in positions which enabled them to manipulate very large sums of money, were reported to the Throne as defaulters, one being in debt to the Company to the amount of 62,000 taels, and the other of 30,000 taels. The Emperor was naturally indignant, or appeared to be so, at these disclosures, and ordered the local authorities to adopt stern measures for the recovery of the money, and to imprison the defaulters until the last tael should be made good.

It is proof of the very large profits which such a company might have rightly accumulated, that even with these and other heavy losses—a later manager showed a deficit in his accounts of 200,000 taels—the affair remained a going concern. Ship after ship was added to the fleet, and in spite of the loss on the coast of six steamers, twenty-six vessels still carry the Company's colours, and may roughly be held to represent about 2,000,000 taels. In the annual report of the Company for 1887 it is stated that during the year the balance of income over expenditure was more than 400,000 taels, and that after deducting the amount set apart for depreciation of steamers, warehouses, etc., at all the ports, there yet remained a balance of 205,000 taels, besides an extra dividend of

20,000 taels, and a bonus to the managers and other *employés* of the Company amounting to 10,000 taels. In those flourishing circumstances the shareholders were paid a bonus of 1 per cent. over the official dividend of 6 per cent. In the presence of these figures it is impossible to avoid the conclusion that with careful management a dividend of twice or three times this amount might easily have been paid.

The experiences of the shareholders of this Company were not such as to encourage others to invest in concerns managed by officials, and when a year or two later Li invited subscriptions to the railway which now connects the Kaip'ing coal mines with Tientsin, he appealed in vain The wealthy burghers refused to invest a cent, and the railway was eventually made at the expense of the Government. Although it is true, as has been shown, that the China Merchants' Steam Navigation Company, though weighted with official control, has proved remunerative, it may fairly be doubted whether any dividends would ever have been forthcoming to rejoice the shareholders, if the Company had not been so strenuously supported throughout its career by Li. By constant manœuvring the Viceroy secured a monopoly of Government freights northwards for the Company, and even so far nursed its interests as to prevent the merchant steamers belonging to the Governor of Formosa from trading on the Yangtsze-kiang, or on the coast north of that river. On this point Li carried on a vigorous controversy with Liu, the patron of the Southern fleet, and so completely overmastered his opponent that Liu was glad to put an end to the dispute by selling his two steamers to the Northern Company. In the same spirit of monopoly Li has strenuously supported the Shanghai Cotton Factories, which owe their establishment to his influence, against all competitors, and up to this time has successfully opposed the importation of machinery by foreigners into the country. By the present treaty with Japan this monopoly is doomed, and the Factories, which will now have to enter the lists against all comers, on equal terms, will probably have a more healthy though perhaps a less remunerative career before them.

It is to be feared that Li's experience of foreign mercantile agents has not been such as to make him regard with tenderness their rights, or to listen with consideration to their appeals. At the close of the war with France, when it was commonly supposed that China would be thrown open to foreign enterprise, he was inundated with applications for concessions, with offers of financial aid, and with tenders for supplying railways, bridges, guns, and other paraphernalia of peace and war. So keen was the competition among financial agents that it was a common saying among Chinese officials that if they only waited a little, money would be offered them without interest; and it was positively stated that one firm proposed to make sixty miles of railway, free of cost, if a certain railway concession were granted to them. The eagerness with which these offers were thrust upon Li made him suspicious of the tenderers, and the avidity with which the competing firms begged for his patronage has probably had much to do with the postponement of undertakings, which, but for this, would have been accomplished ere now.

But Li's attention was by no means mainly occupied at this period (1886) with municipal matters. Two questions of *haute politique* came prominently forward, and in both it became his duty to negotiate for the rendition of lands which it happened were occupied by England and France. After the last outbreak in Korea a widespread fear had existed that Russia had sinister designs on the Peninsula, and the British Government, in order to secure itself against any advance southward from the Amur, occupied the island known as Port Hamilton, off the southern extremity of the Hermit kingdom. In obedience to the following telegram from the Admiralty—"Occupy Port Hamilton, and report proceedings"—Admiral Sir W. Dowell hoisted the British flag over the island. The move was so unexpected that the Powers interested hesitated at first to make any protest. By degrees, however, they recovered their breath, and the Tsungli Yamén expressed their opposition to the continued occupation of the island, on the ostensible ground that if they were to sanction the transfer to the British flag they would be expected to grant compensating advantages to the other Powers. As was usual, the negotiations in this case were mainly entrusted to the skilful diplomacy of Li, who added to the Tsungli Yamén's contention the assertion that the continued occupation of the island might "mar the friendship between England and China." As a more peaceful aspect of affairs had in the meantime supervened, the British Government was ready enough to restore the island; but they felt it incumbent on them to demand from China an understanding that under no circumstances whatever should it ever be handed over to any other Foreign Power. Li was by no means unwilling to take advantage of this condition, to extract from Russia a formal undertaking that she would not at any time tamper with Korean territory. In this he was successful, and, without much trouble, he induced M. Ladygensky, the Russian *chargé d'affaires* at Peking, to give him a definite assurance that, "in the event of the English occupation of Port Hamilton ceasing, Russia would undertake not to interfere with Korean territory under any circumstances." Armed with this pronouncement the Chinese Government were able to give the guarantee demanded by the English Foreign Office, and on 27th February, 1887, the British flag ceased to float over Port Hamilton.

The other important matter which engaged Li's attention was the removal of the Roman Catholic Cathedral, from the position which it occupied inside the Imperial city in Peking, to a site outside the walls. Under the enlightened rule of the Emperor K'anghi (1661–1721) the Catholic Missionaries, who had won the favour of the sovereign by their scientific attainments, were permitted to build the cathedral within the Imperial precincts. Of late years, however, the presence of this church, which considerably overtopped the surrounding buildings, had been a constant cause of complaint on the part of the Tsungli Yamên. The question was a thorny one, and one about which considerable feeling had been expressed. It was eminently one therefore which, if it were to be brought to a successful issue, should be left in Li's hands. Among the foreigners employed by Li was a certain Englishman, named John Dunn, who had on several occasions done his employer yeoman's service. This man Li determined to send to Rome to negotiate with the Pope for the removal of the cathedral. At the same time Mr. Detring, whose name has already been mentioned, and will be referred to again, was commissioned to arrange with Father Favier, on the spot, for a new site on which the building might be re-erected. Both deputies were successful in their negotiations. The Pope sanctioned the transfer, and Père Favier accepted a site which was cordially approved of by the Emperor. As the height of the original building had been one of the main objections to it, it was arranged by this agreement that the new cathedral should not exceed sixty Chinese feet in elevation, being thirty feet lower than the old cathedral; and that the bell tower should not project much above the main roof. This solution of a difficult matter was highly gratifying to the Chinese Government, which showered distinctions on the agents employed in the matter; and a private gift of £7,500 from the Emperor to the Missionaries emphasised the Imperial satisfaction at the conclusion of the negotiations.

IN reviewing the choice which Li has from time to
time made of the foreigners who have entered his
employment, it is satisfactory to find that in almost every
case he has been honestly and well served. Among the
large number who have at different times accepted service,
it could not but be that some should have turned out to
be less loyal to their chief than others. In this connection
the case of Herr Von Möllendorf at once suggests itself.
This gentleman was sent by Li to Korea, to represent the
interests of China at the court of Seoul. With absence
from China the interests of that country seem to have
become dwarfed in the mind of the deputy, and under
the genial influence of the Russian minister at the capital,
he is said to have embraced with enthusiasm the views
disseminated from St. Petersburg, and even to have
induced the Korean Government to form an alliance with
their northern neighbour. It is needless to say that so
soon as this became known Herr Von Möllendorf was
promptly withdrawn, and Korean soil knew him no more.

The negotiation for a loan, which Li entered into with Count Mitkievsiz, who hailed from the appropriate clime of the United States, showed for once a lack of that clear insight into character which commonly marks the great Viceroy. With some few exceptions such as these, it is satisfactory to reflect that the best work which has been done in Li's viceroyalty has been directly due to the skill, energy, and honesty of his foreign *employés*.

It is perhaps not fair to compare Chinese with European officials. The standards of morality recognised by the two classes are so entirely different that it is difficult to make a comparison between the two. Li has a right to be considered as a good specimen of the Chinese official class, and yet we find him in the closest relationship with men who have been convicted of forgery, of malversation of funds, of cowardice, and of bold untruthfulness. It will be remembered that some few years ago a certain Tcheng Kitung, who was attached to the Chinese Legation in Paris, entered into negotiations for raising a loan from the Banque de Paris, which, when they became known to the Chinese Minister, were promptly disowned, and the bank suffered the loss of the amount which it had advanced to the ingenious Secretary of Legation. For this offence Tcheng Kitung was sent back to China, where he was thrown into prison on the charge of fraud. By some unexplained means, however, he was fortunate enough to gain the light of Li's favour, and, under the Viceroy's all-powerful patronage, to recover his liberty.

Another protégé of Li's is the celebrated Chang P'eilun, who now occupies the dignified position of his son-in-law. This officer, as has already been mentioned, behaved so shamefully on the occasion of the French attack on the southern fleet that he was dismissed from his post, and sent into exile beyond the Great Wall. He is unquestionably an able man, and Li's influence, which was freely exercised on his behalf, was sufficient to atone for his past misdeeds, and to restore him to his friends in the Flowery Land. So complete was the alliance and friendship between Li and the ex-exile, that the Viceroy consented to bestow the hand of his only daughter on the returned wanderer. It is said that the young lady protested vehemently against the marriage ; but parental authority in China is as the laws of the Medes and Persians, and, in spite of the tears of the bride, the "happy event" was celebrated with lavish festivities in the autumn of 1888. The admiral who had commanded the fleet at Foochow, and who had offered no resistance to the French attack, had very naturally shared Chang P'eilun's banishment, and the return of this poltroon was a necessary corollary to the release of his companion. Li, therefore, with due consistency, besought the Throne to grant the admiral his freedom, and his prayer was heard.

At the opening of the recent war with Japan, a certain man named Shêng gained notoriety by buying obsolete rifles and inappropriate ammunition for the troops which were being sent to the front. This man had long been, and, if report speaks truly, still is, a prime favourite with Li. He had been mixed up in a number of the Viceroy's undertakings, and had played a conspicuous part in the management of the China Merchants' Steam Navigation Company. A certain blight seems to have rested on most of the managers of that Company. Official has succeeded official with bewildering rapidity, and the new brooms, which were expected to sweep clean, have swept such an amazing quantity of the profits into their own pockets, that instant dismissals have, in most cases, followed the audits of the accounts. Dishonesty has never been a necessary bar to Li's favour, and not long ago he presented a memorial to the Throne, in defence of a cashiered officer, whom he was charged by a Censor with employing at the military school. The officer's record was so bad that the Censor had an easy task, and, on this occasion, even the sheltering power of the Viceroy was insufficient to protect his protégé. With prompt energy the Emperor ordered the defaulter to be sent about his business, in spite of Li's explanation that the inculpated official's action in foreign affairs "was characterised by a judicious mixture of tenacity and laxitude"—a description which would also have applied to his manipulation of official finance. An application made by Li for the services of a cashiered judge from Fuhkien was more successful, and Shêng now follows a less dignified, but possibly not less remunerative career than formerly, in the service of the Viceroy. The constant breaches made in the banks of the Yellow River and Grand Canal are evidences of the very lax way in which Li was served by the officials employed on those works. But his misfortunes in such matters are not confined to the waterways of the Empire. When he first established the harbour works at Port Arthur, he sent a number of native engineers to construct the fortifications. The natural results followed. The "engineers" built walls that toppled over by the force of their own weight, and erected houses that tumbled down of their own accord. At first successful efforts were made to conceal these manifest imperfections, but they were too obvious to be overlooked, even by Chinese Generals, and Li was finally persuaded to employ a French syndicate to do the work for the sum of 1,150,000 taels. Not all those, however, on behalf of whom Li memorialises the Throne, are of the same kidney as Chang P'eilun and others. Old soldiers who fought under his banners during the Taip'ing and Nienfei rebellions constantly receive his powerful support, and lately he petitioned that posthumous honours might be decreed to a certain ex-Minister, Ho Shoutzu, who had been cashiered for an offence which, if so regarded in England, would probably lead to the dismissal of every Minister in the Cabinet, from Lord Rosebery downwards. Being of a studious turn of mind, it was Ho's habit, in moments of leisure, to haunt a certain bookshop, where, while acquainting himself with the contents of the volumes exposed for sale, he established an intimacy with the bookseller. A watchful Censor pointed out in burning language the gross impropriety of a Minister being on friendly terms with a tradesman, who, it was implied, quite after the Chinese manner, had doubtless intended to make use of the Minister's friendship for sinister purposes. Having no powerful friends to protect him against his enemies, the Minister was dismissed from his office, and subsequently retired to Tientsin, where he lately died in obscurity. On enquiring into the matter, in response to Li's memorial, the Emperor admitted that the Minister's fault had been a very trivial one, and, in consideration of his past services, granted, without hesitation, the posthumous honours pleaded for by Li.

It is evidence of the Viceroy's energy and power of initiative that, with the materials he has chosen to employ, he has been able to accomplish so much. It is entirely owing to him that a railway now runs from Taku to Tientsin and on to Shanhai Kwan, and, if he had only been allowed to have his own way, main lines would long ere this have traversed the Empire, from north to south and from east to west. At Tientsin he established a naval school, a military school, a torpedo school, and a medical school, all of which are now flourishing, and all of which have done, in their different ways, excellent work. It was not the fault of the naval instructors at Tientsin that the battle of Yalu was so badly fought, and that the fleet at Wei-hai-Wei did not act more on the aggressive than it did. Nor can the Director of the torpedo school be blamed for the curious inactivity of the torpedo boats in both engagements. The fortifications at Taku, which were undertaken by Li's instructions, are said to be admirably planned and of undoubted strength ; and the drilled troops, which are especially attached to his person, are armed and equipped after the most approved fashions. It is needless to say that some of his experiments were failures. He was persuaded by a French firm to invest in some military balloons, which never did more than gratify the curiosity of himself and his followers. Several ascents were made at a cost of 500 taels each, but before long climatic influences, as it was said, rendered the balloons valueless, and the bubble burst.

Those who remember the old bridge of boats which crossed the river opposite the Yamên occupied by Li, will be grateful to him for the iron bridge which now takes its place, and his attempt at introducing macadamized streets in Tientsin has earned for him the benedictions of all passers-by. In all these innovations he has shown himself to be vastly ahead of his countrymen, and his expressed desire to open mines in Chihli and Manchuria, is proof of his having broken once and for all with the familiar and childish superstitions of his countrymen. Probably in no direction has he shown more complete confidence in modern science than in that of medicine. Twice he has been stricken down with paralysis, and on both occasions he has placed himself unreservedly in the hands of Dr. Irwin, of Tientsin, whose skill and attention he ungrudgingly acknowledged at the public dinner with which he commemorated his 70th birthday, and at which, in all human probability, he would never have appeared but for the skill of his English doctor. It is well known that during these illnesses he was constantly urged by those immediately about him to dismiss Dr. Irwin, and to accept native treatment, with all its manifest absurdities; but neither the persuasions of his friends, nor the superstitious fears which they invoked in the support of their pleadings, moved him for a moment. During the first attack, in December, 1888, he obtained three months' leave of absence, and the Emperor was constant in his enquiries as to the progress he was making, and in his advice that he should secure the best medical aid. Prince Ch'un also expressed solicitude for his recovery, and sent him twenty pills, which had been

especially prepared in the palace, but as he recovered it
is probable that he did not take them.

"Externally," we learn from the *Peking Gazette,* "he
applied a lotion to dry up the tears in his eyes, and
internally he took medicine to relieve his kidneys and
promote circulation . . . The doctor's bulletin states that
the disease is already eight-parts gone. With the mildness
of the spring he will be able to go out once more, and
under the vivifying influences of that health-giving season
his muscles will resume their proper functions, and the
dryness of the mouth will disappear."

Li expressed himself profoundly grateful for the consideration shown him by the Emperor, and assured His
Majesty that nothing was further from his intention than
to take his ease. "Though I have been," he wrote, "on
leave for the past month, I have been daily occupied in
transacting business and seeing my subordinates, and
have often forgotten to take my food until after the going
down of the sun. All through the stillness of the night
my mind has been troubled with the thought that my
sickness might cause some miscarriage of public business."
In reply to this memorial the Emperor wrote with his
own hand, "We have carefully perused the above, and
must again urge upon the patient to be still more careful
in sparing himself anxiety and labour, and to continue a
course of medical treatment, in the hope that his early
restoration to health may remove the earnest solicitude
which we feel on his behalf."

It was just about the time of his first seizure that his
only daughter was married to Chang P'eilun—an alliance
which certainly has not reflected honour on the Vice-
regal house. In his domestic life, fortune has not always

dealt kindly with him. His first wife, with a young family which was springing up about her, was carried off suddenly by death ; and his second wife fell a victim to malarial fever in June, 1892. This lady, who was as gracious and kind as she was clever, was, unlike most Chinese wives, a real helpmate to her husband. She shared his progressive tendencies, and more especially his faith in foreign medicine. For years she was attended by Miss Howard, afterwards Mrs. King, and formed a close friendship with that lady. She established a hospital at Tientsin, which she visited regularly ; and she was instrumental in founding charities for the poor and destitute of the district. She died at the comparatively early age of fifty-six, and her death was mourned by the sick and needy, as well as by those who had been admitted to her friendship.

It was with her approval, and even it is said on occasions at her instigation, that Li took part in the foreign municipal life of Tientsin. In memory of his old comrade in arms he built the Gordon Hall, at the public opening of which he was present. There also he entertained the foreign consuls, and other leading foreign residents, at a dinner which he gave in March, 1892, to celebrate his 70th birthday. On that festive occasion the principal mandarins of the district sat down to a sumptuous repast, in company with the Viceroy's European guests ; and in response to a speech proposing the health of Li, the Viceroy's son, Li Chingmai, responded in idiomatic English. The commemoration of this auspi-cious event extended, however, far beyond Tientsin. The Emperor presented the septuagenarian with a table inscribed with his own hand, together with several illustrated scrolls, the statue of a Buddha, a dragon robe, and sixteen pieces of choice satin. Not to be outdone, the Dowager Empress presented him with gifts of a similar kind, and added a priceless robe, composed of the throat skins of sables.

At the same time an address written by Chang Chihtung, the Viceroy of Hukwang, and signed by a long list of officials, was presented to the man whom they all delighted to honour. In this address, which was written throughout in a style of Oriental imagery, Li was credited, and rightly credited, with most of the innovations imported from Europe. "Your name," wrote Chang Chihtung, "is in men's mouths as was Chou Yen's of old, and you have managed foreign affairs like Hwa Yi. . . . You are altogether admirable, in literature deep, in war-craft terrible, in perception acute, in genius sublime, you are entrenched on every side, unassailable." His work in connection with fortifying the coast was thus described: "Krupp guns protect every river, masked batteries lurk in unsuspected spots, one fort supports another, hills are cut through, towers are raised, soldiers hide within the walls, secret passages provide exit. Possible enemies circle round us, even as the Great Bear round the Polar Star; right and left we face as the changing moon. Let enemies advance, you are protected on every side." The telegraphs, "like the strings of a mammoth monochord," stretch from pole to pole; and "Lantzu's dictum, that the world could be known to him without moving from his study, and Sakyamuni's, that he would circle the globe in a moment,

are now realised." Chang Chihtung is probably, next to
Li, the most prominent man in the Empire; and he winds
up his eulogy by comparing himself to the object of his
adulation in these terms: "As I stand beside you in the
Hanlin I feel how small I am, how little able to grapple
with the great matters met with in my province on the
great commercial highway (Yangtsze-kiang). In you we
have perfect confidence, and I earnestly desire to learn
from you. Compared with you, I am as a simple peasant
to a picked archer, a poor jade to a fleet racer. You are
men's ideal. You, like K'ang Hou enjoy the confidence
of our sovereign; yours is the glory of Chang the
Councillor. You are the cynosure of all eyes." Though
probably with some exaggeration, this paper represents
the feeling of admiration with which Li is regarded by
his friends; and it speaks volumes in his favour, from
the patriotic point of view, that towards the end of his
long career he should still maintain the esteem and regard
of his countrymen.

That Li has bitter and relentless enemies is beyond
question, and the repeated attacks that have been made
upon him by the censors show that, though he has
hitherto been able to withstand their assaults, they have
not given up all hope that they may yet be able to
accomplish his downfall. One of their last onslaughts
was a cowardly stab at him during a period of great
affliction. In his anxiety to show all respect to the
memory of his wife, he surrounded her funeral with every
manifestation of woe, and lavished unbounded sums on
the funeral *cortège*. For this he was fiercely attacked by
the censors, who instanced the expenditure of this money

as evidence of his having overstepped the line of official honesty. The attack signally failed, and the inculpating memorial was treated with silent contempt.

Li's willingness to join in the promotion of the welfare of all local concerns, whether undertaken by natives or foreigners, has made him popular with all classes of society; and after the recent dastardly attack on his life in Japan, this feeling found expression in the following telegram, which was forwarded to him from the members of the Tientsin Club: "The foreign residents of Tientsin offer sincere sympathy to His Excellency. They deeply regret the calamity which has befallen him." To this message Li returned the following answer: "Thanks to all for kind remembrances. Wound painful. Bullet cannot be safely removed, but am improving steadily, and can attend to business from bed. My best wishes to the whole community.—Li Hungchang." The readiness with which Li has always received foreign visitors has already been remarked upon, and his outspokenness on such occasions, when he has a purpose to serve by it, is proverbial. Some few years ago Mr. William Jones, a delegate from the English Peace Society, presented himself at his Yamèn. Li received him hospitably, and listened to all he had to say. He expressed surprise that Mr. Jones should have come to China to advocate views which had always been those of Chinese statesmen; and he reiterated the assurance that his government was then, as ever, pacifically inclined, and would never fight unless compelled to do so. Having thus expressed the virtuous attitude of China, he went on to advise Mr. Jones not to call the righteous but the sinners to repentance.

" Why don't you attack the grasping policy of Russia ? "
he said, "and why don't you go and preach righteousness
and justice in St. Petersburg ? " Recent events have
shown that Li was right in both views. China has fully
demonstrated her unwillingness to fight, and there have
not been wanting signs that Russia's grasping policy has
lost none of its keenness.

IN the course of his long career, Li Hungchang has seen many vicissitudes. He has basked in the sunlight of Imperial favour ; he has suffered from the frost, the killing frost, of his Imperial master's displeasure; he has been held up to the admiration of the nation as the one man who could save his country from its enemies, and he has over and over again been denounced as a traitor to that country by intriguers and sycophants. In all these varying conditions, in the midst of his friends and in the face of his enemies, he has maintained with unflinching courage an equal mind and a steady course. In the case of one who has worked with such unflinching devotion in his country's interest, it might have been hoped that towards the close of his career his repeated applications for leave to retire might have been granted, and that his declining years might have been relieved from the anxieties of the affairs of State.

It not infrequently happens, however, that as the

VICE-ADMIRAL ITO
(of the Japanese Fleet).

bodily strength diminishes, the Fates delight to concentrate their attacks on the aspirations and powers of those who through a long life have defied their assaults. So it has been with Li Hungchang. The crowning trial of his life, and the severest test to which his courage and his policy have been put, were reserved until he had lived beyond the common lot of man ; and he who, through the whole course of his administration, had regarded the Japanese with special contempt, was destined when he was two and-seventy years of age to sue for peace at the hands of the *Wojên*, and to accept the terms which in their day of victory it pleased them to dictate.

It was well known to all those who had watched Eastern politics that affairs in Korea had for a long time been in a very critical state. The numerous reforms which had been proposed by the Japanese and adopted by the king had been consistently thwarted by the Chinese party at the Korean Court. It was impossible that the constant friction engendered by this state of things could last indefinitely, and last year matters came to a crisis. Disturbances broke out in opposition to the reforming policy of the Court, and the situation was complicated by the Chinese, in contravention of the terms of the treaty of 1885, landing a force without giving notice at Tōkiō of their intention to do so. From the Japanese point of view the position had now become intolerable. Not only was there a powerful political clique representing China at Seoul, but an army had been landed to add force to diplomacy. In this emergency the Mikado despatched troops to the Korean capital, to give countervailing support to the King and his advisers.

Li was not alone in his recognition of the "grasping policy of Russia." Japanese statesmen had long been apprehensive of a Russian invasion of Korea, and it was this fear which added zeal to their desire to see radical reforms effected in the peninsula. A weak Korea, they knew and felt, must always be a temptation to Russia and a source of danger to Japan, and they determined to seize the present opportunity to set in motion such reforms as would give strength and efficiency to the Hermit kingdom. Li, in common with the Tsungli Yamên, was entirely misled by the Chinese representative at Tōkiō as to the temper of the Japanese on this question of the day. Their sharp political controversies had led the Chinese statesmen to believe that the Japanese house was divided against itself in foreign as well as in domestic politics. But though in the House of Representatives the different cliques quarrelled over the army and navy estimates, and the principles of popular representation, they were united in their determination to secure the Empire which they had built up, against the grasping policy of their northern neighbour. Once and for all, they were determined so to reform the institutions of Korea as to constitute her an effective Buffer State. With this object the Mikado's Government, in a spirit of friendly alliance, proposed to the Tsungli Yamên that they should conjointly undertake the necessary changes in the administration of the peninsula. To this proposal Li replied that as China was the Suzerain State, any reforms in the country must be undertaken at her instigation, and under her supervision. Li was unquestionably anxious to maintain peace; but when he took up this position he

entirely misunderstood the attitude of the Japanese
nation, and even made the mistake of presenting an
ultimatum at Tōkiō, demanding that all Japanese ships
should leave the Chinese ports before the 20th July. To
this injudicious document Japan returned a conciliatory
reply, but, at the same time, warned the Chinese Government that, under the circumstances, any advance of their
naval and military forces would be regarded as an act of
war.

In spite of this very plain intimation, Li despatched the
British ship *Kowshing*, loaded with troops, and escorted
by three men-of-war, on her way to Korea. On the 25th
of July this convoy encountered the Japanese cruisers
Akitsusu, *Yoshino*, and *Naniwa*. The result of the
encounter is well known. The transport was sunk, and the
Chinese war-ships took to flight. Following this disaster
to the Chinese arms came in quick succession the defeats
at Asan (July 30th), and Pingyang (September 15 & 16);
and the naval battle of Yalu (September 17), at which
the fleet commanded by Admiral Ting was vanquished,
though after a hard fight. At first the news of these
disasters was kept from the Imperial ear. But the truth
came out at last, and Li, who had been held responsible
for the success of the campaign, was degraded in rank,
and stripped of his Yellow Jacket and Peacock's Feather.
Li saw now, when it was too late, the mistake he had
made, and strongly advocated the adoption of peaceful
counsels. But the Emperor and his advisers, in their
ignorance of the true relative position of their country,
were not yet convinced of the futility of continuing the
contest. Events, however, soon brought conviction to

their minds. Day after day adverse news arrived from
the front. On October 25th, Marshal Yamagata crossed
the Yalu into Manchuria. On the 31st he captured the
important city of Fènghwang Ch'èng, and three weeks
later the Japanese flag was hoisted over the forts of Port
Arthur (Nov. 21).

The fall of this stronghold was a crushing blow to Li
Hungchang, who had superintended its growth from
the time when it was a small fishing village to its
development into a mighty fortress. People are pro-
verbially proud of their own creations, and he had
fondly hoped that Port Arthur would be able to turn
back the tide of war, even should it be against the
attacks of European armies and navies. Meanwhile, in
response to his urgent representation, an Imperial decree
was issued, directing him to send Mr. Detring, a Commissioner of Customs, to arrange terms of peace with the
Mikado's Government. This proposal was strictly in
keeping with Chinese action on previous similar occasions. Any other nation in such a position would have
despatched a highly-placed and fully accredited native
Ambassador. But with that haughty contempt with
which China has always professed to regard Japan, a
foreign Commissioner of Customs was considered quite
competent to deal with the emergency. The following
letter, which served as Mr. Detring's credentials, illus-
trates the attitude which Li, in common with the
Emperor's advisers, adopted, at this time, towards their
conquerors :—

"Earl Li Hungchang, Imperial Commissioner, &c., to
his Excellency Count Ito, Minister-President, &c.—The

Ta Ching dynasty is in the enjoyment of its traditional policy of peace with every nation, but there have lately arisen, unhappily, disputes with your country whereby the usual friendly intercourse has been exchanged for a state of war. Seeing that no inconsiderable calamities have lately fallen upon our people, it is now proposed that both countries should temporarily direct their forces on sea and on land to cease hostilities. A memorial having been presented to the Throne as to the advisability of this course, the commands of his Imperial Majesty, my august master, were received as follows :—

"'Whereas Mr. Detring has held office in our Empire for many years and has proved himself faithful and true and worthy of the highest trust, we command Li Hung-chang to inform him fully and completely of whatever has so far been deliberated upon and decided, and to direct him to proceed to Japan without delay and effect a settlement. As occasion arises Mr. Detring will inform us confidentially, with due speed, of the progress of the negotiations.'

"In accordance with his Majesty's commands, Mr. Detring, together with officials holding rank of the first grade, is directed to proceed to Tokio to present this despatch and to learn the conditions upon which peace may be regained and amicable intercourse re-established as of old. I therefore request your Excellency to discuss with Mr. Detring the manner in which friendly relations may be restored. This despatch is written commending the proposal to the favourable consideration of your Excellency."

Accompanying this despatch Li sent the following private letter to Count Ito, with whom he had long been on terms of intimate friendship :—

"In the year 1885, the 11th year of the reign Kuang Hsü, when your Excellency honoured me with a visit in Tientsin, we negotiated a treaty whereby the Eastern question was settled upon a basis calculated to insure permanent peace to our respective countries. Such a solution entirely captivated my heart, and caused that treaty, when duly signed and sealed, to be regarded as the guarantee of eternal peace. Never was there a momentary anticipation that within my own lifetime would arise such a deplorable state of affairs as now exists.

"In the early stages of this present complication, venturing to hope that matters might be amicably arranged and extreme measures avoided, my endeavours were strenuously directed towards effecting a pacific settlement, but the sudden outbreak of hostilities, casting aside all treaties, to my extreme grief, excluded every peaceful alternative. Since then time, with its full measure of calamities, has rolled on, and I never cease to ponder over the peace I so earnestly desire between our two countries.

"Victory and defeat are necessarily matters of uncertainty; the end is difficult to foresee. Should war with its resultant misfortunes continue year after year, assuredly the people will become impoverished till a state of complete exhaustion supervenes. Such a proposition needs no extraordinary intelligence to comprehend it, and it is because I recognise its vital importance that I now endeavour to reopen the question, in order that our two countries may come, if possible, to an understanding.

"Having memorialised the Throne, the commands of his Imperial Majesty, my august master, have this day been received to send Mr. Detring to wait upon your Excellency, that he may convey and make known my sentiments. During his long and faithful service in this Empire, Mr. Detring has repeatedly been entrusted with the conduct of difficult affairs, and my Government, as well as myself, place in him the most implicit confidence. He is thoroughly conversant with the circumstances and conditions that obtain in both our countries, and is imbued with a deep conviction of the advantages of peace and the disadvantages of war. Your Excellency may remember that he acted as my adviser in the negotiation of the treaty.

"My request is that your Excellency will favour him, as my trusted friend, with an interview. I look anxiously across the seas, straining my eyes gazing toward your Excellency's distant home, feeling that time cannot have effaced the memory of our former intercourse; it must remain graven upon both our hearts. More might be added, but what has been said will serve to manifest my heart's desire, and I avail myself of this opportunity to express the hope that your Excellency may enjoy well-merited happiness."

[Card of] "Li Hungchang,
"November 18th, 1894."

In both of these documents Li showed that he entirely misapprehended, or chose to misapprehend, the position which an ambassador should occupy, and it is difficult to understand how Mr. Detring could have consented to undertake so bootless an errand. If he had ever been under the impression that his mission was likely to succeed, he was quickly undeceived on his arrival in Japan (Nov. 27th). He had no sooner landed at Kobe than he was courteously informed that his credentials were insufficient, and that the Japanese Government could not recognise him as a duly appointed envoy. The object of Li in sending Mr. Detring was obvious. If the Japanese could have been induced to accept him as an ambassador, he might have succeeded in getting favourable terms from them, when he would have received the full support of the Chinese Government; but in case of his being forced to accept such conditions as were unpalatable at Pekin, the Tsungli Yamen would have at once thrown him over as not being a properly constituted ambassador. The rebuff given by the Japanese Government to this disingenuous manœuvre was therefore

richly deserved, and the question next arose what further
step was to be taken. The failure of this embassy and
the consequent discomfiture of Li, were considered by his
enemies to afford a fitting opportunity for a further attack
upon him, and a memorial signed by over a hundred and
twenty Chinese officials, bringing charges of corruption,
peculation, and deception, against the Viceroy, was presented to the Throne. This attack, like so many others
that had preceded it, failed in its object ; and Li's
position was strengthened by the fact that he was taken
into council by the Throne on the subject of the embassy,
which it had again become necessary to send to Japan.
After much deliberation two Mandarins, Chang Yinhwan
and Shao Yulien, were appointed to negotiate terms of
peace with the Japanese authorities. On the 26th
January these ambassadors started on their errand, in the
Empress of Japan, for Yokohama. Not even the Detring
fiasco, however, had taught the Imperial Government
the meaning of the word "plenipotentiary," and it was
perversely thought sufficient to furnish the envoys with
the following meagre credentials :

"We hereby appoint you to be Our Plenipotentiaries,
to meet and negotiate the matter with Plenipotentiaries
appointed by Japan. You will, however, telegraph to
the Tsungli Yamen for the purpose of obtaining Our
commands, by which you will abide. The members of
your mission are placed under your control. You will
carry out your mission in a faithful and diligent manner,
and will fulfil the trust We have reposed in you. Respect
this."

It is almost needless to say that so soon as this
document was submitted to the inspection of Count Ito,

the Prime Minister, and Count Mutsu, the Foreign Secretary, they at once recognised its insufficiency, and declined to open negotiations with the Chinese ministers.

Fortunately for China, Prince Kung had already been recalled to power, and in him Li found an active and energetic supporter. In accordance with Chinese usage, the failure of Li, to whom the conduct of the campaign had been entrusted, to keep the enemy from the gates had entailed, besides the loss of his Yellow Jacket and Peacock's Feather, the withdrawal of all military affairs from his control. His advice, however, was eagerly sought at Peking, and it was to him that the Emperor eventually turned in his sore difficulty. While others had been found wanting, he alone had proved himself comparatively trustworthy, and his Imperial master now determined to place the destinies of the Empire in his hands. His knowledge of affairs, his high standing, and his unquestioned ability pre-eminently marked him out as the man of all others who could now save his country in her dire need. Though an old man, and worn out with cares of State, he yet consented, at the earnest desire of the Throne, to visit for the first time in his life a foreign country, and to undertake a humiliating mission, which must have been as gall and wormwood to his proud nature. Recognising the patriotism which actuated his acceptance of this post, the Emperor restored to him all his honours, and, further, appointed him a special Imperial Commissioner to conclude peace with Japan. This was on the 15th February. On the 7th the stronghold of Wei-hai-wei had fallen; and the telegram which brought the news to Europe of Li's appointment announced the suicide of Admiral Ting, who having defended Wei-hai-wei with marked courage, if not with strategic ability, had refused to survive its fall.

Respect is undoubtedly due to the memory of this gallant officer. Both at Yalu and at Wei-hai-wei he showed a brave front to the enemy, and it was only when all hope of a successful resistance had disappeared that he negotiated for the surrender of the fortress. A correspondence, which has survived him, does him infinite credit, and shows that he was a patriot, as well as a gallant sailor. Admiral Ito, who was commanding the Japanese fleet at Wei-hai-wei, and who had long been on terms of personal friendship with Ting, wrote to him, with doubtful morality, urging him to come over to the Japanese until the conclusion of the war. Ting declined this invitation in simple and dignified terms, and when a few days later Admiral Ito sent him a present of some champagne and other wines, Ting replied by letter, "I have to express gratitude for the things you have sent me, but as a state of war is existing between our countries it makes it difficult for me to receive them. I beg to return them herewith, though I thank you for the thought." On the 12th February Ting took poison, an example that was followed by his second and third in command. With fitting courtesy, Admiral Ito did honour to the memory of his late gallant opponent by detaching a despatch vessel to carry the Admiral's body, with respect and honour, to Chefoo. It was with a knowledge of these events that Li, after having been received in repeated

audiences at Peking, left Taku on the 16th March for
Japan. On the arrival of Chang and Shao on Japanese
soil, there had been something like a hostile demonstration
on the part of the natives; but it was universally felt,
even by the most heated partisans, that Li's position was
one which entitled him to every courtesy and respect.
Both by Counts Ito and Mutsu he was cordially greeted
on landing, and, in company with Mr. Foster, his
American adviser, he was escorted with every manifestation of respect to his hotel. After the first preliminary
meeting of the Plenipotentiaries the business under discussion advanced rapidly. Li had, in the first instance,
urged that an armistice should be granted during the
continuance of the negotiations. This the Japanese
Plenipotentiaries were ready to agree to, on condition
that the Taku forts, Shanhai Kwan, and the railway
thence to Tientsin should be handed over to the
Japanese generals in the field. These terms, however,
were too onerous for Li to accept, entailing as they did
the virtual command of Peking; and the Plenipotentiaries,
therefore, at once proceeded to discuss the terms of
peace. At the third interview matters had progressed
favourably, and there had appeared to be every prospect
of an immediate conclusion of peace. At its close,
however, an event occurred which altered the whole
complexion of affairs. As Li was being borne through
the narrow streets of Shimonoseki to his hotel, a member
of the Soshi class, who are to the modern Japanese what
the Ronins were to the people in the pre-reform days,
rushed up to his sedan chair and fired a pistol point-
blank in his face. Happily the powder was of a kind

which commonly accompanies cheap cartridges intended for foreign use, and the bullet, which entered a little below the left eye, failed to penetrate to any great depth. The dastardly assassin was instantly seized and imprisoned, and by none was his act more sincerely repudiated and condemned than by the Mikado and his Ministers. By Imperial command the Court physicians were sent at once to attend on the Viceroy, and Count Ito called in person to express his deep regret at the brutal outrage.

With the true instincts of a high-minded statesman, the Mikado felt that some public act was necessary to give expression to the national abhorrence of the deed, and he directed his Ministers at once to grant an unconditional armistice, which was to last till the 20th April, and which, as a matter of fact, was ultimately extended to the 8th May. It is a happy characteristic of the Chinese that fever seldom supervenes after a wound or an operation, and though the shock to Li's frame must have been very great, the effects of the wound were probably not so serious as they would have been in the case of a European under similar circumstances. Li shares to the full the aversion of his countrymen to surgical operations, and, contrary to the advice of the doctors, he refused to have the bullet extracted. Notwithstanding this revolt against medical counsel he was, in an astonishingly short space of time, sufficiently recovered to attend to business; and on the 17th of April he signed the treaty of peace on behalf of his Government. At the conclusion of this ceremony elaborate courtesies were exchanged between the Plenipotentiaries, and on the same afternoon Li embarked on his return to China.

In the course of the negotiations Li had been obliged to consent to the main demands of the Japanese, and stress of circumstances had compelled him to append his signature to a document which ceded the Liaotung peninsula (including Port Arthur), Formosa, and the Pescadores, to the conquerors, and by which he further bound his country to pay an indemnity of 200,000,000 taels for the expenses of the war. These terms were recognised as being so burdensome that a strong party at Peking were opposed to their ratification. Li, however, with the help of Prince Kung, was powerful enough to obtain the Emperor's approval of them, and at midnight, on the 8th of May, the ratifications were exchanged at Chefoo by subordinate officials of the two Powers.

But though by this treaty China, and Li, as representing China, were humbled to the dust, they had yet one arrow left in their quiver. They had been obliged to agree to terms dictated by Japan; but it remained to them to effect by diplomacy that which they had been unable to bring about by the force of their arms. By skilful manœuvring at the European capitals they succeeded in ranging Russia, Germany, and France in line for the protection of their threatened territory, and in response to the remonstrances of these Powers, they have now recovered the ultimate possession of Port Arthur and the Liaotung peninsula.

It is impossible to bring this sketch of the life of Li Hungchang to a close without expressing admiration for the courage, consistency, and desire for mechanical

reforms, which have characterised the career of the great
Viceroy. But in the minds of all impartial observers,
this admiration must inevitably be modified by a regret
that, despite his great abilities and his great opportunities,
he has never been able to free himself from the narrow,
bigoted, and warping system which has bound his
countrymen in chains for countless generations. Nothing
he has heard, nothing he has seen, nothing he has read of
Western lands, has served to shake for an instant his
implicit belief in the ineffable wisdom of the founders of
Chinese polity, or in the superiority of the civilisation of
China over that possessed by any other nation on the
face of the earth.

By the exercise of his senses he has had it borne in
upon him that in science, and in the mechanical arts,
more especially in those relating to warfare, foreign nations
have far outstripped his countrymen ; and from his proud
and narrow outlook he has imagined that by possessing
himself of the appliances invented by Western peoples he
would, without doubt, succeed in placing his country in a
position of power equal to theirs. He forgets, or he is
ignorant of the fact, that the most perfect machines and
the most destructive weapons are powerless for good
unless the hands which wield them are guided with
skill, energy, courage, and experience. To him the
long chapter of history which embraces the nations'
struggles for light and leading, and in which may be
traced the growth of a civilisation based on the solid
grounds of religion and morality, is as though it had
never been written. He recognises the value of the
product, and believes that, by grafting it on to the

Chinese stock of blighted and decaying wood, it will bear fruit of equal value with that it brings to perfection on its native stem. With all his acumen, he has failed to understand that this is impossible, that one cannot put new wine into old bottles, and that if his countrymen are ever to stand in line with the leading nations of Europe, it must be by the same processes by which they, through much tribulation, have achieved greatness.

PLYMOUTH:
WILLIAM BRENDON AND SON,
PRINTERS.

A SELECTION OF

BLISS, SANDS & FOSTER'S

𝔓ublications.

S. R. CROCKETT.

BOG - MYRTLE AND PEAT: Tales
chiefly of Galloway, gathered from the years 1889 to 1895. *By* S. R. CROCKETT, Author of "The Stickit Minister," "The Raiders," etc.   Large Crown 8vo, cloth, gilt top, 6s.

"Mr. Crockett has done nothing better; few have done so well."—*Scotsman.*
"Delightful volume . . . admirable and powerful story-telling."—*Glasgow Herald.*
  Will increase his reputation."—*Daily Telegraph.*
  The good wine that needs no bush."—*Yorkshire Post.*
  Weird, pathetic, picturesque, and fascinating."—*Aberdeen Journal.*
"The great reading public that has already taken Mr. Crockett to its capacious bosom will revel in its pages."—*Dundee Advertiser.*
"It is refreshing to find that our age can still produce a book like 'Bog-Myrtle and Peat.'"—*Christian World.*
"The preface and the epilogue are prose poems."—*Daily News.*
"Racy of the soil to an eminent and altogether delightful degree. —*Aberdeen Free Press.*
"Strong and artistic work . . . the majesty of the hills is in the book."—*Leeds Mercury.*
"Excellent from cover to cover, and will certainly increase the number of Mr. Crockett's admirers."—*Speaker.*
"It is like coming on a purse of new bright sovereigns."—*British Weekly.*

CHARLES T. C. JAMES.

ON TURNHAM GREEN: being The
Adventures of a Gentleman of the Road. *By* CHARLES T. C. JAMES, Author of "Miss Precocity," "Holy Wedlock," etc.   Crown 8vo, cloth, 6s.

"We have not been so glad of anything for a long while. A refreshment to our middle age."—*Daily Chronicle.*
"Is wholly charming."—*Standard.*
"Humour as well as pathos."—*Scotsman.*
"Gay and gallant tale."—*Daily News.*
"Very acceptable reading indeed."—*World.*
"A galloping story."—*Saturday Review.*
"Lively, fascinating, and romantic."—*Manchester Guardian.*
"Worthy of Dickens."—*Aberdeen Free Press.*

HELEN P. REDDEN.

M'CLELLAN OF M'CLELLAN.
By HELEN P. REDDEN.   Crown 8vo, cloth extra, 6s.

MONA CAIRD.

THE DAUGHTERS OF DANAUS.
By Mrs. MONA CAIRD.   Third Edition.   Crown 8vo 480 pp., cloth, 6s.

"Mrs. Sarah Grand's diatribes are mere milk and water compared with Mrs. Mona Caird's indictments."—*Standard.*

LONDON: BLISS, SANDS AND FOSTER

www.ingramcontent.com/pod-product-compliance
Lightning Source LLC
Chambersburg PA
CBHW030358270326
41926CB00009B/1171